TESTIMONY OF A POET

Bruised by Angels

Melanie Goodall Hightower

ISBN 978-1-63961-753-1 (paperback)
ISBN 979-8-89130-981-4 (hardcover)
ISBN 978-1-63961-754-8 (digital)

Christian Faith Publishing
832 Park Avenue
Meadville, PA 16335
www.christianfaithpublishing.com

Printed in the United States of America

I dedicate this book to God first and to my mother who had suffered pain and long sleepless nights praying. To my children, Joshua James Watterson, who is my firstborn, Dashawn Louden, second child, and Atiya Monique Hightower Osteen. May God's blessing be upon you, three children, who I really adore and love. It's my desire to prove to you God is real and able to bring you all through whatever obstacles get in your way. May God bless you all always. Remember there is no failure in life but lessons and stepping stones to learn. Seek to please God. Only your soul is important. To my two sons, listen to your Father God's instruction and do not forsake your mother's teaching.

Contents

Bible Verses

And it came to pass men begin to multiply on the face of the earth, and daughters were born unto them. That the sons of God saw the daughters of men that they were fair and they took them wives of all which they chose. (Genesis 6:1–2)

The interpretation of Genesis 6:1–4. The interpretation of Genesis 6:1–4 is difficult and controversial. The debate centers on the interpretation of the phrase "sons of God." Who are they? The crucial question concerns whether the phrase refers to human beings or to spiritual beings (demons).

The Lord speaks of his people as jewels. (Malachi 17 KJV)

And he cried out with a mighty voice saying, Fallen. Is Babylon the great she has become a dwelling place of demon and a prison of every unclean spirit, and a prison of every unclean and hateful bird. (Revelation 18:2)

And another angel a second one followed, saying Fallen, fallen is Babylon the great, she who has made all the nations drink of the wine of the passion of her immorality. (Revelation 14:8)

Revelation 18:24. After this, I saw another coming down from heaven having great authority, and then earth was made bright with His glory. He called out with a mighty voice, "Fallen, fallen is Babylon the great. She has become a dwelling place for demons, a haunt for unclean bird, a haunt for every and detestable beast. For all nations have drunk the wine of the passion of her sexual immorality, and the kings of the earth have committed immorality with her, and the merchants of the earth have grown rich from the power of her luxurious living." Then I heard another voice from heaven, saying, "Come out of her my people lest you take part in her sins lest you share in her plagues, for her sins are heaped high as heaven, and God has remembered her iniquities."

> Thus says the Lord God, "This is Jerusalem I have set her in the center of nations with countries all around her. And she has rebelled against the nations and my statutes more than the countries all around her for they have rejected my rules and have not walked in my statues." (Ezekiel 5:5–6)

> They were nations about which the Lord had told the Israelites You must not intermarry with them, because they will surely turn your hearts to their gods Nevertheless, Solomon held fast to them in love. (1 Kings 11:2)

> Surely the Lord does nothing without revealing his plan to his servants the prophet. (Amos 3:7)

Introduction

This book is introduced to the crack addict, alcoholic, heroin addict, prostitutes, and all those that are addict to sex. I invite you to read this book that is design by God to let you know He has not forgotten you even though you made bad choices but were stepping stones. There is no failure just lesson to learn.

In the book of Genesis, it speaks how sons of God looked at beautiful women, and they took the women of men and went to bed with them. These women bore children unto them. This was a sin. These angels were disobedient angels who left their position, which was there spiritual body. God cast them into dark places for judgment, and Satan who became the head over these angels got crafty and summit drugs, which is witchcraft, and cause you to break the law of God and Christ and steal your soul through the birthing of the women who bore children unto them.

I know God chains them in darkness and destroys that generation of those who became giants after these women who bore children unto them, but He did not destroy those angels. Using drugs, Satan took us to darkness with him. He carried our spirit into darkness, which he needed our body to perform his dirty works, stealing, lying, cheating, and so on. We would say we were bless when we trick someone out of their money with the craftiness of Satan. But the Word told us to try the spirit by the word of God and tried the word by the Spirit.

The book of Revelation 2:9 and Revelation 3:9 show how God is calling those to repent and come out of Satan's synagogue, and that is how it all happened. God had impregnated some of you with the same message He has given me to conceive and give birth. But some of you probably aborted the child, believing that it was not of God.

We intend with these angels by using drugs and sinning, which we separated our self from God, but there was light in darkness because of God planned for Jesus Christ to break the curse of those who intend with these disobedient angels from us through His Son Jesus Christ, who is, in darkness, shining so we could see what God is showing us.

I know there were men who were very old, living in darkness with drugs for a long time, and that is how God's light showed me who they were. Jesus is waiting for all those who believe He is the Son of God, so these angels would be chained down forever and destroy once God get all His children out of the darkness.

I remember there was a time the court put me in a shelter for ninety days, and after ninety days, they were supposed to put me in an apartment. I was still using drugs, and we had a curfew. We had to be back at the shelter, and I met a couple of guys who said I could go to their place and smoke. I knew some of them, and I didn't have a reason to fear them doing any harm to me. It was early in the night. Satan got into one of their minds, and he tried to get crafty by offering me drugs for sex, and it seemed as if my eyesight got really dark, and time seemed to be close to daybreak. I knew at that point I miss the curfew at the shelter, and I would get put out bad as I wanted a hit. I jumped up and left. I went uptown in the part that was not dark, and there were two white women standing in front of a coffee shop. I asked them the time, and they said it was eight o'clock. I knew then Satan took me to darkness. Who knows? Satan could have used one of them to kill me.

"*I made it!*" I like to share with you also that angels don't make themselves known, but there were men women would meet, and they would tell them they were their angels. Those were wicked men. Also, I knew it would be a wicked spiritual being in me because I would hate when daybreak catch me up early in the morning, chasing drugs like AMP. God is supposed to greet you in the morning. I, the word of God, would cause me to remember how God questions Satan and asks him, "Where is thou goes?" That is what I would feel when God would catch me in the early daybreak. I remember the angel that was wrestling with Jacob. He had to be gone by daybreak

that's why he hit Jacob in his side, so Jacob would let him go. I was
blessed by many angel that would come to rescue me in dark places
and lead me out. The word of God said He would send His angels to
take charge over you, and He did.

Joshua

Conceived in my womb, he fought the great battle of humidity of the poison of Satan's drugs I used. Mental disorder, that old filthy turban, was place on his head.

The day Joshua came to present himself, Satan and angels came also to attack Joshua by accusing him of the way he was born with his mental behavior.

His heart was fixed in the conception of my womb, the making of his body God knew.

But the God of creation and the host of Jesus Christ order Satan and his angels to back off while God reclothes Joshua.

The filthy turban was removed and the filthy garment from the battle he fought in my womb.

Royal God spoke and said, continuing on Joshua, the battle is won, obey My laws and decrees and follow in the ways of My Son, Jesus Christ.

Oh, the victory was given to me after the birth of my son.

Remember salvation forgiven from your sin and the consequence your son, I give to thee Joshua.

Written by Melanie Hightower

The Testimony of This Poem "Joshua"

I conceived Joshua out of wedlock, and I used drugs through the whole nine months I carried him. Upon discovering I was pregnant, I asked God why He allowed me to conceive while I was on drugs. God saw fit to respond and said to me, "You conceived in sin."

Before Joshua was born, I decided to name him Joshua not knowing his name means "God is salvation," and salvation means "deliver from sin and its consequence."

The year he was born, it was the law that a child can be taken from the mother if drugs were found in the child's system. Being that my mother thought the way of the law, she went to the hospital with the knowledge I was an addict and asked the doctor to check to see if Joshua had drugs in his system. They did upon the request of my mother, and the results were negative.

My son was release to me. I did not bare the consequence of sin, which was the meaning of Joshua's name. From that point on, I knew God had ordained and chosen me in my mother's womb. Still today I believe God performed miracles, and His ways are unseen but showed to the people He has chosen for a purpose just how He spoke to Moses face-to-face through the burning bush that didn't burn. Miracles still happen today. Joshua suffers mental disorder.

There were relatives that call Joshua mental retarded. It was Satan and his angels, but Satan fail to realize that Joshua fought in my womb. Today Joshua is a minister. He understood the King James Bible better than he understood school assignments. He has many gifts, such as prophetic, computer knowledge, and playing drums. I believe he is going to walk in Kirk Franklin shoes. He has proved to his mama the lies and the curse people spoke over him that the victory was won with the chosen purpose of God Himself. Amen.

My Son's Healing

There was a season of my life that I didn't truly understand what God was saying, but now I see envy, hate, anger, and resentment was going on way before I conceived my son.

I stood proud to the master, requesting, "Will you let me break this curse from thee?" I heard him say to me, "True motherhood perfect bond from the womb I will see you through."

My motherhood wasn't taken from me, that is what society submitted in my son's heart and mind but not his soul. The soul is mine. God rebuked Satan and said to me.

God, the author of my faith, planted the seed of righteousness of love, joy, peace, and long-suffering in the belly of my womb way before he was born or taken from me.

The name Josaphat never follows the ways of Balaam; he will become a Christian truly in God's holiness.

The enemy of this world came along and planted seeds of hate, bitterness, strife, and rejection and placed in the inward fleshy part of his mind that blinded my child until the day he was healed.

Wept many tears, he cried unto me and recognized he came from my womb. I was his mother. He was healed by the shedding of many tears; a perfect bond we did receive on the day my son was healed.

The Testimony of the Poem "My Son Healing"

My second child, who was born eight years after I gave birth Joshua, was taken from me after birthing him because of drugs in his system, but I did get him back at the age of three. He is a very handsome fellow. I remember lying on my side. I was about four months, and a vision dropped in front of my eyes. A vision was being opened. That is why it was a vision, but this vision was supernatural, not a vision of a thought. It was God Himself with a light-blue color telling me to call my child, Josaphat, and tell him never follow the ways of Balaam.

I was in a Pentecostal church rehab, and there I was baptized with the Holy Spirit manifestation of speaking in another language. I was in prayer when they brought my son to me. He looked at me and immediately reached out to me to hold him. His spirit identified me as his mother. After leaving the program with my son, he resided with me and my mother in her home. My son stayed close by me. Even though family members felt I was spoiling him, that was the philosophy that was taught to me through many generation by religious teaching. There was a time he got up out of the bed with me and went to sleep in another bed. The Holy Spirit spoke and said he is wean.

My son got everything he needed from me, and that is when the devil came to take him back from me with lies, hate, vindication, and rejection, but to let you know, it was all in the plan of God the Creator of all things through the seeds of hate and rejection. The bond was broken by Satan's evil devices through family members, but the day of my son's healing, those character traits disappear. The perfect bond that God promised me is what I want to share with you. It was my desire to raise my children different from how I was raised, being that I was raised by the philosophy teaching of religious leaders which God placed in my heart, but I had to understand it was a bloodline curse in order for me to see.

No one taught me to keep my virginity and the importance of keeping it and about charming men was deceit. They only were charming you to see if you were gullible. The meaning of Balaam is cited as a type of avarice for example in the book of Revelation 2:14. Balaam tried to put a stumbling block before the children of Israel to eat things sacrificed unto idols and to commit fornication.

Here today as I write, my son is in a relationship with an Asian girl, and she don't worship Christ, but her father is a Christian, and her mother is a Buddhist, and she follow the ways of her Buddhist mother. Now being Christian, God has a plan for my son that I was not aware of, but upon learning who Josaphat's origins was originated was, Buddhist which God caused him to be attractive to this girl, my son's bloodline were of the bloodline of Buddha, but being born as a Christian

into a Christian family, his purpose is for me to convert his Asian girlfriend to a follow the way of Christ.

After reading upon Josaphat, who was a prince and his father was a king whose name was King Abenner, and he was Indian, which is my birth mother's side of family, whose grandparents were Indian, which is the bloodline who persecuted the Christians. The astrologers had foretold Josaphat would one day become a Christian, so the prince Josaphat was kept in confinement by King Abenner to prevent that from happening, but Barlaam, who was a helmet of Senaar, met him and brought him to the true faith, which his name mean Christian. Saint Josaphat lived the rest of his life as holiness. So I don't fear him in this relationship with this Asian because God told me he would never follow the ways of Balaam. He surprised me when I thought God didn't see my pain and suffering for my son.

I've Fallen So Deep in Love with You

I've fallen so deep in love with you until I can't see nothing but the
thought of loving and being with you, which is all I see. It exists in
my heart, soul, and mind, hypnotizing, memorizing, and consoling
my every me. Wanting, needing to be touch by you. I've fallen
so deep in love with you, drowning in the sea of love, floating on
ecstasy after being rescued by you, freely feeling and breathing your
breath all over me, the breath of life rejuvenating my soul, heart,
and mind. I became alive because I've fallen deep in love with you.

Written by Melanie Hightower

The Testimony of "I've Fallen So Deep in Love with You"

I wrote this poem based on the fact that all I went through, God showed me I had wrong motive in seeking Him and serving Him that it was another reason for the thorn to be placed in my flesh, but today I have arrived to only know that for Christ, I live and seek only to please Him, not for material things. I love God with all my heart, mind, and soul.

Journey to the Heart of My Husband

Journey to the heart of my husband was a very dark day of sorrow, not seeing hope for tomorrow.

Frustration in my mind was the luggage I carried and not knowing the reason I carried so many, until I heard the voice of heaven say, "Let's travel." It was God, my heavy-load carrier.

I was bored in the hands of His care flying wings; He carried me to see the heart of my husband. I begin to see the truth be renewed in me.

As I bored in heaven, I saw eyes looking into me. This man's character was clothed in me.

Wealthy merchants of love, servants of kindness, a steward of gentleness, were presented to me "husband." I saw his destiny was to redeem me.

I struggled to make my plot because the journey to my husband's heart was my battle day and night coming into the marvelous light.

Suddenly I release the baggage of despair rushing trying to get there.

Wealthy merchants of love were given to me servants of kindness to serve me a steward of gentleness to guide me.

Journey to my husband's heart was Jesus Christ.

Written by Melanie Hightower

The Testimony of "Journey to the Heart of My Husband"

This poem was written based upon a time in my life. I carried a lot of issues, which portal the person I really was. I always had the attributes of Jesus Christ but struggled with self-esteem and trying to please people, friends, and relatives. When I first met my husband, I didn't understand why he was attractive to me. He seemed as though he would be attractive to sensuous women. I felt as though he had a motive, but we did get married. My husband was a very gentle and kind man. God used him to direct me to character of Jesus Christ.

I Wish I Were My Husband's Wife Again

I wish I were my husband's wife again. Lying in the arms of his protection only to hear him speak and say I love you. Kissing, caressing, taking me in, touching my face, stroking me his fingers to feel. I wish I were my husband's wife again. His verbal demands my esteem to rise appraising me my value undenied. I wish I were my husband's wife again, nowhere to walk among adulterous nor sin, temptation of man. Burning my core nature demands, dare I take more. I wish I were my husband's wife again. Reason—plenty, wanting, needing, awakening in me to be my husband's wife, his friend, yet lover again.

Written by Melanie Hightower

The Testimony of the Poem "I Wish I Were My Husband's Wife Again"

I was inspired to write because after the separation of my husband, I realized I was wrong as a woman confessed to be a Christian, not realizing God was the head of my husband, and he did ask me to marry him, knowing I am a Christian, which he thought that I would know he was the head, but I was just controlling and bossing, and a Christian knows that they are supposed to be submissive unto their husbands.

The Garment of My Husband

Strength was the tassel cloth on a woman's appearance, which was fashion designed on both shoulder's length tips. Oh, catch this beautiful symbolic slip. It was thin, but it was attached to his inner strength that cover the muscular of a man. So when you see the garment of my husband, you see the formality of me

Written by Melanie Hightower

The Testimony of the Poem "The Garment of My Husband"

This poem was written being that I was a woman, and the woman is the weaker person in marriage, and the garment was Jesus Christ. It took me a long time to grow, and anything that takes long to grow is strong, and Jesus Christ was the garment of my husband.

The Skillful Maestro

The skillful maestro who played the violin so well took me upon the thirty-first floor, upon the roof there. I was with the skillful maestro who played the violin so well.

He laid me down as though I was asleep by placing me in a trance, by looking into my eyes as if my eyes were his music sheet. He was a skillful maestro who played the violin so well.

He made sounds that no violist could make. He made a sound of moans and groans as my body applauded him as if my body was the audience that set within him a skillful maestro who played the violin so well.

Upon the roof there, I was with the skillful maestro who played the violin so well.

Written by Melanie Hightower

The Testimony of "The Skillful Maestro"

There was a time in my life that I was battling with the sin of lasciviousness because at this point of my life, God was showing me what entered the family bloodline, the sin from sons of God "lasciviousness," and he was not just calling me, but he was choosing me to set me apart for himself, but being as Jonah, I rebelled and went on Skid Row. God chases those he loves and chooses. So I continue being on the streets of Skid Row, Downtown Los Angeles, house of Babylon, house of demons, dwelling place for using crack cocaine.

Well, there was this guy who would stalk me and chase me, offering me drugs to lure me into sex with him, but I wanted to heed to the purpose of Christ because many are called, but few are chosen, so I would reject him, but I first had to learn and experience to see what God was really showing me, which was how filthy this sin was.

Through the years of my younger adulthood until my womanhood through fornication, that spirit grew strong in me and became a stronghold, but I had to learn a lesson that didn't come with a test. It came with a purpose, but anything that takes long to grow is strong like a tree.

So fornication was not just fornication for me because God chose to break this curse off me even though it entered through my children. They don't have to tell me, but I know, so I am standing in the gap for them and interceding for them, so Satan had to come through this guy to give himself his best at me to try and cause me to lose my soul because we know in the New Jerusalem, this spirit lasciviousness cannot enter, and with this spirit lasciviousness in you, when you're died, you will enter the second death, which is the lake of fire.

God knows His children just as He knew Job, so I finally saw what God was showing me about this nasty spirit lasciviousness, and I had to learn to hate it. I finally did after that experience on the roof with the skillful maestro.

Clothed in Beauty

Sitting, waiting, still in the midst of her spirit, she waited for the bridegroom to come near. Matrons of honor presented her the most valuable of earrings she was clothed with listening.

The finest jewels were placed around her neck; she was cloth with obedience by the master's request.

Threads made of gold her garment could never be torn; she was clothed in heaven by the hands of the potter.

Oh, how her garment was put together, her seamstress threaded it with strength, and there she was clothed with her inner strength. In her beauty, the lilies of the valley release her to be free, and the leaves clap their hands as she walks through the garden to enter into the royal king palace.

Written by Melanie Hightower

The Testimony of "Clothed in Beauty"

The testimony of "Clothed in Beauty," the earrings was symbolic as listening, which most women don't see that listening is beautiful on a woman, but God ordained me when He built my inner character on these things, listening and being obedient unto him.

The Beauty of Your Love in Me

The beauty of your love in me is when I look into the mirror and see the noble crown upon you and me. The beauty of your love in me is the reflection of your spirit that saturates me. The beauty of your love in me reflects the pureness of white doves that the brightness in my eyes shows the softness of your true love. The beauty of your love in me always surrounds me even when you don't have to tell me you love me. The beauty of your love in me is like an eagle that soars so high above that's the beauty of your true love.

Written by Melanie Hightower

The Testimony of "The Beauty of Your Love in Me"

There was time in my life when I was fighting for my daughter before they illegal adopted her, so I went to rehab named Propatype and stayed six months, then graduated after six months later, then went to college and got my degree for paralegal and got my associate's degree. This is where Jesus manifested Himself in me. My eyes were so white. It was Jesus. There where light in my body that manifested through my eyes after relapse. After I found out, the lawyer I hire filed too late to get adoption turn over. I recognized after meditating that it was Jesus in me. I stayed happy all the time. It was not a time I fell into depression. I was grateful, and Jesus is love. There was no resentment, anger, envy, or strife. I learned to love myself, and that how I found Jesus, I was fearfully made whole.

Looking for Jesus

Looking for Jesus in the churches or the sanctuary of Christ or the Catholic belief in the touching of the rosary cross when He is right there in your heart as close to thee you are. When you close your eyes and search deep within, you will see Jesus.

Looking for Jesus, He is the man on the curb with the homeless begging for bread.

Are you looking for Jesus? He is there in the sick, begging you to just lay hands to heal the spiritual dead man.

Looking for Jesus, He is the hurting father wanting you to just understand about his adulterous wife that it wasn't just a fight.

Looking for Jesus, He is there on death row, waiting for a saint to listen while He mourns through true repentance before the death angel carried Him home.

Looking for Jesus in all the wrong places when through this poem, I just painted His face.

Written by Melanie Hightower

The Testimony of "Looking for Jesus"

At this point in my life, I decided I wasn't going to a drug rehab or anything of that source if God was God who created all things, and He knew my lifeline and formed me in my mother's womb. Surely he could supernaturally deliver me, a power that was greater than drug programs being I was constantly relapsing by the principal of this world (rehab system) of what they taught.

I landed downtown in Skid Row. I remember the first day in downtown. I woke up from sleeping on the sidewalk, and I had an accident on myself, my monthly period, and I didn't have a change of clothes. There was this clothing store across the street from where I was sleeping, and there was a voice that spoke to me that told me to go over there. It was the Holy Spirit, so I did as the spirit directed me. I entered the store and spoke to who I thought was just the salesman, but coming to the knowledge, it was the owner whose name was Michael.

I explained to him that I had an accident on myself, and I needed a change of clothes. His mother and father were standing next to Michael. All three of them, for a brief moment, looked at me as if they were having an intervention with God, then the mother spoke and said, "Let her look for something to wear the clothes." I picked out clothes given to me.

Michael and his family were very kind to me for over a two-year period of time. Never once did they make me feel I was wearing out my welcome. If I needed money for food, it was given with shoes for my feet as well.

There were many people God used to help me with my needs. Never once did they question me and ask me if I was on drugs. The word of God came to me and said love and kindness. I have drawn thee, but I didn't understand how God still loved me when the drug addiction was going still, but coming to the knowledge, it is what rehab and some Christian made me feel. Rehab caused me to fight in my own strength. The word of God also said He will send His angels to take charge over thee, and if I acknowledged Him in all my ways, He will direct my path, so I learned these people who I came in contact with me saw Christ who never left me or forsaken me. He taught me love through it all and gave me the gift of love and faith. I've learn to give my last by trusting and being able to meet my own needs. Amen.

Desperate Hope

Desperate hope how I wait wanting to manipulate, but the earth shake, warning me to wait, knowing the testing of my faith brings perseverance, patience, and the greatest faith that won't shake.

Desperate hope is just a seed as small as a mustard seed that speaks in my ears, "My child, please wait."

Desperate hope will turn to faith just open up and learn to appreciate the testing of your faith without complaints, holding on every step of the way, knowing God is the author and finisher of your faith.

Written by Melanie Hightower

The Testimony of "Desperate Hope"

This poem was written when faith became strength after God showed me I was manipulating people when I got arrested and had to serve time. I manipulated mainly my mother while I was in jail. After I acknowledged the correction from the Holy Spirit, God sent people in my cell that would offer to buy my needs and wants. "Praise God!" So faith became rooted in me as small as a mustard seed.

Look into Your Heart with a Positive Mind

Clear the attack of the enemy from that filthy turban that came to blind you of who you really is casting down every imagination and thought pulling down strongholds, letting go of everything you left behind, men who tried to blow your mind with smooth-talking words that stole your virginity and dump you into a world of sins because he never meant to marry you.

So now take hold of the faith you always knew when you were fashioned in your mother's womb and look into your heart with a positive mind and find security in Jesus Christ, who is so divine, the man, the comforter, and the gentlemen. He won't trick you into the immorality of a bed of sin to steal your virginity and self-esteem.

God has given you beauty deep within that was fashioned in your mother's womb, a strong woman, wealthy in character to win many sons and daughters, with your lamp stand standing, filled with oil that will never go out but will burn sinful men and sinful women if they tried to come near but only for you to wait for Christ.

You will find Him if you look into your heart with a positive mind. There you see His purpose after being deceived by that serpent Satan's immorality, sinful men and women that came through the bloodline just to try and steal.

Remember as you go your way, the journey is narrow but choose Yahweh's way. You must walk alone. Beauty is passing, charm is deceit, but a woman of God shall be praised.

Written by Melanie Hightower

The Testimony of "Look into Your Heart with a Positive Mind"

When I was in junior high school, there was this guy who was very popular because he was cute and handsome. I will never forget he offered to walk me home after school. I was amazed because I was a nerd. Had I known that sons of God came as young man, they would continue to be born and birthed even after being placed in darkness for the Day of Judgment because people will go in dark places and party and use drugs and drink liquid and sin. Women will bear children for these men, and that is how the curse came about. When God told women not to marry certain men, He has a divine revelation for the reason we should obey.

Well, I accepted this guy's offer, and when we got to my house, I asked him to wait at the door. I entered into my house to my bedroom, and when I turned around, he was behind me. He pushed me to my bed and proceeded to get on top of me. I pushed him off me with force and told him to get out and never come back.

He left, and I was so ashamed, and there was no one that was around me for me to be ashamed of. The shame came from hurt, seeing his lust after the out beauty of me not who the person I was. That was my first lesson and intervention with God, showing me He designed me long before my mother conceived me to be a women of God, but I came through a bloodline of curses.

When sons of God looked at beautiful women, they took them and had sex with them, and they bear children. Yes, God did destroy that nation, but as I wrote in the testimony earlier, they came about again through women being disobedient in dark places, but God's plan was greater for me to reach out to young men and women and tell them to hold their virginity and not to be flattered by charming boys or girls, which is deceitful.

I lost self-esteem that day, and I always thought to go the way other boys and girls went, which is sex, to hold on to whosoever I thought will love me. But through life, they took my inner beauty—Christ, which manifested on the outside, but the word of God said beauty is passing, charm is deceit, but a woman of God shall be praised, and just to mention, it was not the out beauty they saw, it was inner beauty that sons of God saw—character.

When I Used to Live Downtown

When I used to live downtown, I never looked down at all the sinful men and women all around because I knew Jesus died for my sins, and He was taking me through to learn a lesson only He can give and to build my heart for His people who I never could find until I live downtown. When I lived downtown, I didn't look down on the beggar man or the sinful women who had the bottle in her hands. His disciple I shall be, but a woman of God only designed by thee. Hypocrites! I did look down on the high-lifted and self-righteous. Never once did they see me or Jesus Christ who died for my sins. Now I see how the Samaritans came about and the sinners who accepted Jesus Christ because the church folks belittle me and Jesus Christ.

They sent rums, Pharisees who were blind because of their filthy garments, cloth around their heart, fearing unclean when it was seen in them. They hid in filthy garments in their public works. Never once did they lay hands on the sick or blindmen. He couldn't see Christ in the fake Christian man who crucified Christ on Calvary cross.

Every day, they crucified me, not seeing it was Christ carrying me. The beauty I saw in Christ is why didn't they see. They would have seen Christ who they crucified in my flesh, and because I was looking through the eyes of me, if only they could see me through my eyes, which they couldn't look inside because of the sin they had in them. They knew they were hiding, and the brightness of true love would have blinded them.

When I lived downtown, I was a student wearing my crown. A shepherd Jesus shepherded me and taught me to lead the blind with love, and they would see. Oh, how my heart bled with tears when I learned my part. "Love," he kept telling me no matter what. Whether it be a testing of your faith, keep love. I don't want to be like the hypercritics and the Pharisees worrying about Satan trying to deceive me in my faith. Love cast demons out.

I learned through Christ when I lived downtown, I would rather have Jesus than silver or gold, the filthy turban and garments Jesus striped off, what the Christian put on me, false teachers that didn't have love.

When I lived downtown in Skid Row, I gained my crown. Oh, if they could have seen the Christ that lived in me, they would have come and rescue me with the laying of the hands and casting out demons with true love. I learned a lesson from above when He came through those. I looked up in their eyes and saw Christ's true love, so I never looked down when I lived downtown.

So I bless those who gave to me without a title but with true love and kindness. He drew me when I lived downtown. A title is just a name, but when you search and read and see the fruits, the title means nothing because with true love, you don't see it. It doesn't need praises. That's not from above. Only praises from men, they were looking for. So I learned a lesson that was well taught. Seek to please God. Trust no one. When you don't see true love, it is Jesus Christ.

When I used to live downtown in Skid Row, I was a student of love. I heard a minster say a message from Calvary one day, not knowing I had to crucify flesh and receive the power of love. No one told me in the Christian faith that love came with power. The day the Holy Spirit came upon me, Jesus said, "I will receive power, and it didn't come with blessing of materialist things. It came in the long run after long-suffering, rejection, being talked about misjudge, and belittle the tithe he gave me was love after coming from downtown. Out of the church of babies "Corinthians," he has chosen me when I live downtown in Skid Row.

Written by Melanie Hightower

The Testimony of "When I Used to Live Downtown"

This was a great experience for me, and I was for sure in a secret place with Jesus Christ. I learned how the hypocrites, sinners, and Samaritans came about. There were people who came as missionaries as they said they were, but they worked under organizational names so as to say they were helping the homeless, but there were no one concern about the homeless healing sores on their legs, etc. But God showed me the ones that proclaimed Christ had sin in them; they couldn't cast out demons in Jesus's name because of the sin in them, but I recognized that the people was covered by Jesus's blood who were homeless on the streets.

That is why I know through all I went through, God showed me it was not going to be known, one who came to lay hands on His sheep that were scattered all over the land because of the wicked shepherds. His Son Jesus would deliver them like me. I came out without an incurable disease and also the ones that really backslide the world. God told the angels it was Jesus who carried the seven stars in His hands. God told them to speak to the angels at the church and cause them to return those in Satan's synagogue to return and to come out of Babylon as well.

I Almost Died in Sin

I went to Downtown Los Angeles, the city of Babylon Egypt, a dwelling place where I was rejected by my family there, not knowing I was chosen for Christ. Hurt and in pain, I said to myself I will dwell here in Babylon Egyptian dwelling.

I build up my forts and place a tent as my resting place, forgetting about Jehovah Jeru, the man who crucified the flesh.

Self-pity, I found myself in, so I said I will dwell here in Babylon with the sinners. I feast on drugs, booze, and fornication, trying to medicate the emotional pain that really was divine, forgetting how to pray when I was ashamed.

My heart hardened against God. Kidney called my name "failure" to keep me from going to the pits of hell. God got my attention on the bed of my sickness. I almost died in sin.

Written by Melanie Hightower

The Testimony of
"I Almost Died in Sin"

All through the years, I became weary in trying to demonstrate Christ in my family, but my motives were wrong. I was loving my family more than Christ when He was trying to set me apart. I discovered I had kidney failure, and I was ready to die because I felt I didn't have a life living by a machine three times a week, and I was tired of fighting drug addiction, so I went on the street of Skid Row to die, but God delivered me by His own hands from drugs supernatural, and the kidney failure He kept as a thorn in my flesh to bring me back to His eating laws, which He chose me to be set apart.

I am still alive as I write, and this is the way I will be able to reach my family by expressing in my poems after every lesson and victory despite of everything the devil did to me from my childhood through some of my adult life, and my family could see God had me in a secret place even on drugs, which they didn't understand what I was seeing or the visions God was showing me because it was not His time as I look back. It was Satan, his angel, and the Lord of Host at war when I would tried and explained to them what I was going through, and they would rebut against me. God used even strife for good. There was an angel who kept the secrets of God.

I remember me as a baby in Christ; there was this prophet named Jonah who came to me and said, "You like to share." I said, "Yes, I do," but he was not talking about material thing, and he knew that is what I was thinking. He said, "Not that you can't share everything. God says you might be putting it in the hands of the devil." I still did, but God also used it to show me who was against me in my family.

Dysfunction

Were you ever raised by a single parent without the father? Well, society and philosophy said this is dysfunctional, but through this poem of portal, I am here to let you know that is not so. America, you see, was a nation that didn't marry no one, but born children, unwed, outcast. She was kicking in her own blood, trying to live. God passed by her and spoke to her and blow the breath of life on her and said live because no one had pity on her because of being dysfunctional. God became the head of her and the Father of her children because she was a weak woman, not because of dysfunctionality.

She trusted her own beauty, and every man that would pass by her with the wink of the eye, she went to bed with them and bore children unto them and didn't cause one of them to marry her. God called her Jerusalem, weak woman. So you see we called her children crack babies and drug babies. God said she caused His children to go through the fire, which she conceived in lust and weakness, giving everything to her lovers what God gave to her.

Oh, this was not a small matter unto God, so before you, philosophers, psychologists, teachers, false prophets, and college teachers, who teach a lie, a lesson you haven't learn, or know the real true knowledge of Christ, let's stop cursing what can't be curse. Jerusalem, "Oh, America," who the United States is "bless" of, not dysfunctional she was, but if you want to teach the truth, tell your student about crack babies and drugs dealers. They are the children of America, who was a women that went to bed with many different nation and never made one nation marry her, but she was blessed. God built her and gave her the best of everything from His very own.

Let's not teach dysfunction. Dysfunction is an illness of a body part that don't function properly. God is the head of every living thing. He is sovereignty and all mighty, and all power is in His hands. So if you say the United States is dysfunctional, so be it because they are American, but blessed. I was born and conceived by a married woman, still religious, teach taught, and said I came from a dysfunctional family because my daddy wasn't there. Let me tell you the truth, my mother gave me everything I needed as God gave to her love and use her to demonstrate a woman of true character that not to be weak and gave herself to Satan. His worshipers are dysfunctional because we need Jesus Christ, God's son, to function properly, but remember dysfunction is the dysfunction of an organ.

The Testimony of "Dysfunction"

Well, coming in school, I learned that my family was dysfunction because both parents were not there living in the home together, but after learning in the word of God in the King James Version Bible, I came to find out that was not so. Jerusalem was an outcast, and God saw fit to receive her and cause her to be beautiful and gave her the best of everything, but like I mentioned in the poem, she trusted in her own beauty and went to bed with many nation of different nationality and bore children for them, but they were God's children. She cause them to go through the fire because of not being married to their father. They went through many hardship and trials like myself, but God was my Father, and I was well raised by him, and to top it all off, dysfunction is someone birth with a physical organ that is not functioning properly.

Backslider

You called me a backslider, Christ chose me out in secret place when they thought I arrived, but in the church, I conceived and had to birth in an open field out of the church, so next time you see me, you will surly say she have birth Jesus Christ (Israel).

The Testimony of the "Backslider"

Years ago, before I came to write this book, there was this woman. Prophecies came through her to tell me she saw in a vision the moon and the stars were under my feet. I didn't understand her vision until now. Also, before she would tell me this, it would be seven stars I would see at night over my head. When I was on the streets, no matter what side of the city I would go, they would always be over my head.

Now the woman in Revelation 12:18 was the woman who gave birth to Jesus, and He was taken into heaven unto God after she gave birth, and the woman flew unto the desert where she was fed for so many years, which was the nation Israel, which it was revealed to me that it was me. Because God first spoke to me before all of this took place and told me not to eat the swine, I grew up on pork, but when I read this, my spirit absorbed what I was reading, and I knew God was telling me not to eat the swine. He chose me unto the nation Israel. Now I have been feed and clothed on the streets of Skid Row, which was my desert, but foreigners it was beheld Jesus in them. They didn't wear a title. It was Christ, which the women of Israel birth, so God chose me out of the church to birth Jesus Christ, which is "love," and enter into His laws and decrees such as a royal nation like Israel.

Two Travailing Sister

Two travailing sisters didn't walk side by side or kneel in prayer together but were in one body. Only one knew the hidden revelation who carried her as well as she carried me to be birth for a set time. One was the one who carried the seven spirits like Mary Magdalena. What a deep mystery of the two travailing sister. Couldn't it be the new Jerusalem? That is morning to be birth when you would think it was the younger sister who the older sister would birth but the scapegoat. The baby sister was the one who would give birth to the older sister, but oh, how close they were like Siamese twins. Don't feel sorry or look down on Siamese twins. They are God's angelical, spiritual beings. When you see it in the revelation of God, heavenly beings, when, oh, if you could see the beauty of the two travailing sister.

Written by Melanie Hightower

The Testimony of
"Two Travailing Sister"

I have a sister. We are a year apart. We talk alike and sound just alike. One day, she was over my house, and I had a friend there visiting me. She was in the bedroom, and I was taking a shower. The Holy Spirit came upon me, and I was speaking in tongues. When I got out of the shower and got dressed, my friend asked me who that was praying with my sister, which, through my friend, he confirms the question it was my sister praying through me. But I know, but I don't know if my sister is aware of this, but it is a deep mystery of Christ.

Rekindle

Rekindle my spirit, Lord, so the fire in my soul won't burn against those who did me wrong.

Rekindle my heart, Lord, so I could enter Your gates with thanksgiving.

Rekindle the Holy Spirit so that your word would reach many.

Written by Melanie Hightower

The Testimony of "Rekindle"

The testimony of this poem is how God healed me from anger against some of my church members, friends, and the pastor of a church I once attended, and family members humbled me to accept the things they spoke against me and wrongfully did to me and by me forgiving them, and His reward was His Son Jesus who I seek only to please.

A Man Instructed Me

On a full moon, late one dark night, through the knowledge of Christ, angels came through the city to destroy those who continually disobeyed God.

Who could that being be who spoke to my inner ethical me. A man instructed me to abide under the shadow of God's wings. I have been redeemed.

Thou the angels of death tried to come near, I have been guilty of many sins. Caught in darkness late one night on a full moon, I cried out loud in fear of God, "God, please forgive me." Suddenly a man appeared and said to me, "Go, sin no more." He instructed me with a full spiritual force of Christ.

The Testimony of
"Man Instructed Me"

This is my testimony of how death was on me. It didn't matter with all the knowledge and gifts I had from God, it would have turned me over to the death angels. I knew it was God because God controls the spirit world even when Satan thought he stole the power from Adam in the garden. God still overpowers Satan by controlling the spirit world. When I took a hit of rock cocaine, I began trembling and fearing. I remember that God said in Revelation 2:1–5, God speaks and said how He will come quickly and take or remove my lampstand quickly if I didn't repent, meaning under the influence, death angels would have struck me down. I immediately left Skid Row and return to God.

Singing Fire

All night long, as I slept, I heard the singing fire singing to me. Could it be King Solomon of songs? No, I will go see.

It's my Lord. Where couldst thou be? I could hear His voice where couldst thou be?

Standing at the city gate, there with my eyes, I search where couldst thou be? My Lord, please kindle this fire inside of me. My spirit carried me to the valley to look for my Lord. Where couldst thou be? I saw nothing but thorns and bristle and fruitless trees. Where couldst thou be? This fire is burning inside of me.

Come, my love, and find me. I feel your desire to hold me. I promise I won't run, flee, or escape from thee.

I know I will go to my bedchamber of marriage where we once drenched myself in sweat after lovemaking. Sure, he will be there waiting for me, and there he was as I entered with Christ, the comforter being the center.

There I saw Jesus anointing me and with the oil from Zion came, my love, my friend, I want to carry you over the threshold where we could begin again.

It is I who must carry you through the storms of life; the singing fire
you felt inside was the touch of the master's hands to allow me to be
in demand.

Now you see this singing fire will always be only to be kindled by me.

Written by Melanie Hightower

The Testimony of the Poem "Singing Fire"

The testimony of this poem is how God brought me back to where He first baptized me with the Holy Spirit and His Son, Jesus Christ. That singing fire was the Holy Spirit that's why I searched downtown in Skid Row, and I saw Jesus in the people who gave to me and did not judge me, which caused me to come back without having to go to a drug rehab. God's way was perfect; He had a chosen a purpose for me. Fruitless trees as you read in the poem were symbolic, meaning people, churches, and rehab that blessed each other but rejected the brokenhearted and the outcast that lived on the streets. Bedchamber of marriage is symbolic for when I first got baptized in the Holy Spirit and prayed in my holy languages, while God burned all the impurity out which I sweated.

Hurricanes of Withdrawals

When I *sleep at night, hurricanes of withdrawals try to whirl me in and take me back to the pits of hell of dragons and demons where Satan dwells.*

Tossing and turning all through the night, drench with sweat confused in my mind.

For ninety days, every night I went through withdraws of hurricane dreams.

But early one morning, when I rose, I heard the voice of the book of Job getting my attention in a vision of a dream, not to return to the streets of LA, that old devil Satan's den.

Those hurricane of withdrawals finally ended those visions of dreams.

I got the victory through the testing of my faith. Confused no more from the book of Job.

The Testimony of the Poem "Hurricane of Withdrawals"

After me getting off drugs, I had many nights of nightmares of getting high, being tormented by the devil, making me feel as though I wasn't delivered off drugs, trying to make me feel. I still had the desire. But in the book of Job, it speaks about how God get our attention in a vision of dreams to warn us not to return, keeping us from going to the bottomless pit of "hell" (Job 33:15 KJV).

Entreaty

Please hear my supplication. I plea for an earnest request at the master's quest. Redeem me, I promise I will hearken to your will. It's your voice that entreats me to come near so I could plead to thee. Earnest is seeking through prayer earnestly, I request, I won't let entreaty have no rest.

Written by Melanie Hightower

The Testimony of "Entreaty"

Through this poem "Entreaty," I was begging God to deliver me from drugs even though I had sobriety, but I was not yet delivered from drugs. That spirit was hiding in me, and I knew, and I call it a drug demon which those he was pastor of drug rehab lay hands on me, but I knew I was not delivered. I still desire to use, but I kept on going on the principal of the drug rehab rules to sobriety. It worked for so long. I remember my mother telling me, "If you are delivered, why do you have to continue to go to meetings?" Because she would have to set important things, she had to do to take me and pick me up. I knew she spoke the truth, but I didn't want her to know I was praising the leaders at the church and putting them on a pedestal, but God saw fit to take me through all that I went through to birth Jesus Christ in me and in my heart. Now I seek no other but Christ and only to please him. I was getting sober to gain custody of my children and to win my husband unto Christ. I was seeking God for wrong motives.

I Am That I Am

I am who I am. The question you ask in your conscious mind speaks the truth to yourself all the time wondering if I am God. I am that I am. I am walking with you every step of the way even when you think I left you behind. I still answer your question. I am that I am. You ask, could this be God that is taking me through? I am that I am every step of the way

Written by Melanie Hightower

The Testimony of "I Am That I Am"

Long as I remember, I would be speaking to myself, and now that I have been fully grown in the knowledge of God, I know His voice, and it was God Himself I always was speaking to through the Holy Spirit.

Under the Wings of My Mother

Under the wings of my mother was the garment of her robe hidden; she me under her wings were the things she once trodden down.

She knew my steps. Every step of the way, she knew Satan came to test her faith. She was the woman that conceived me.

She beheld me close to her breast. "Oh," thee she was the eagle that sow so high above that flap her wings, beckon me to run under near, from the beast and the crows of the field.

"Oh," how I obeyed and stayed near under her wings until the enemy of the field flew away.

Even when I went astray, I found myself learning great things she once knew and gained the victory over Satan's evil devices who

came to test her siblings and her younger offspring.

When the battle was over, she flapped her wings, beckon me to come from under her wings and find rest.

Under the wings of my mother, I was redeemed.

The Testimony of "Under the Wings of My Mother"

This poem I wrote explains how I never left my mother's cover until I grow strong in the Lord Jesus Christ, and after I did, I found perfect peace in Christ and learned to rest in him. Oh, how it was a battle for me and my mother fighting my drug addiction, sleepless nights she bore, but the victory was won through many prayers. We won the battle. Our relationship is perfect in Christ Jesus. This is my testimony. It was worth the fight.

I Say I Do

I know you knew it was true when you looked into my eyes. You saw I love you although you tried to run and hide because the pain of hurting me came as no surprise. You fought hard to keep me away, but God came in to build our faith. So let's hold on to God's unchanging hand because only God can see us through. One and one equal two. Don't you see? You are for me. We were meant to be. Life is meaningless without a wife. So I say to you I do.

Written by Melanie Hightower

The Testimony of the
Poem "I Say I Do"

I wrote this based on marriage decision I had to make but was afraid of marrying the men I truly love. He had everything I look for in a man—smart, intelligent, and kind—but he was a womanizer, but I did marry him, and God prove Himself to me because I knew he was just that, a womanizer.

Praising the Saints That Are Not

Living for the people in the church, the so-called saints that are not, when you know that something isn't right, but you keep on pretending they are right "just to praise them" just to fit in. This was not right praising the saints that are not. The living word of God is calling true saints to go out by the highway and byways and restores the lost at any cost. Did you hear God calling your name by your spirit and proclaiming you to come out? Has he chosen? You are just called your name from among the saints that are or isn't? Did you answer are? Did you conceived Christ the Son of true love that was on fire burning in your spiritual womb.

I will lure you to the valley, but you kept on praising the saints that were not when it was Jesus you were supposed to conceive and birth him in an open field but afraid this was just a delusion of a vision, not of a dream. But not now, you were called to the valley to birth Christ, the lover you needed to enter the New Jerusalem, where there you won't congregate with the saints that were ant's. This wasn't a vision of dream, it was Christ who stirred you up no matter. Whether you turn to the left or the right, He wouldn't let you rest until you birth Christ. For nine years, you carried the seed of Christ. For "crying loud," I was in labor. I must deliver true love if I was going to lay hands on the sick, the brokenhearted, and the least fortunate. This is what God has chosen me to do, not prosperity.

I cried loud in travailing, moaning to birth this child out in an open field. I birthed Christ after conceiving him in the church. It was Jesus who was looking for a heart of God to go down in the streets to bring His sheep out of the captivity of Babylon, lost in her bed of immorality, but these men crept in the church with the immorality of sin in the pulpit and the great whore who sits upon their heads. I had to be led by the Spirit, and God lured me to the valley to birth Jesus Christ, now true love. I receive power to lay hands on the sick, cast out demons in Jesus's name, the brokenhearted, and the outcast to be restored to Jesus Christ. I praise God only, not the saints that are not.

Written by Melanie Hightower

The Testimony of "Praising the Saints That Are Not"

I was baptized by the Holy Spirit in a church that was a church of babies, but I knew there was a power operating in me greater than what the teachers were teaching. They laid hands on me and say I was delivered from drugs, which was many years before I wrote this book, but it was not true. I wanted to say I don't feel delivered. I know feelings are not real, but when God did it, I did not have a desire. God wanted to birth true love in me, Jesus Christ. This is where the power was with love, no love, no power. I knew demons were not going to come out when there was no love in the person who was doing the laying of hand on. I wasn't confused. I knew they wanted the people to praise them, knowing they were babies, and these teachers prey on them 'cause most of them scatter all over the land, so God came through to choose His true vessels to come out. I was called by my heart, not by my name. He had given me a new name, Anthelia. God shall be exalted. I was chosen to exalt God only, not praise men for their selfish works and to see the power of love by laying hand on the unclean to cast out demons. I birthed Jesus Christ in downtown Skid Row in the spirit. I saw the message God was showing me about His people, the Gentiles, that still need a savior.

The Thorn in My Flesh

It was something that was going on with me that I didn't understand. It was a thorn in my flesh. I heard Noel Jones saying to me. I know he doesn't mind me using his name in this poem to lift him up in the presence of God who sits on His throne, and I knew it was God's misting spirit. This thorn in my flesh kept me relapsed to keep me from thinking I was better than others, keeping me from exalting myself above measure because of the many gifts God has given me. In the church of Corinthian, "babies" testing only on milk when we should have been eating the meat because our digestive system was design and prepared to digest the true, even if it was bad news and required true repentance.

I prayed continually to God, "Please remove this thorn in my flesh," but when I go to do right, sin would present himself, and I would do wrong. It was sin that was in me, trying to buffet me up beyond measure. Who could deliver me from this thorn in my flesh? Not even a pastor, preacher, or teacher could explain or instruct me on what to do with this thorn in my flesh, not even lay hands on me to cast this thorn out of my flesh, but, oh, how Jesus was crucified. They placed a crown of thorns on His head and pierced Him in His side. It was Jesus who went to Calvary cross with this thorn in my flesh and died to crucify the flesh and was keeping me from being buff up.

It was Satan trying to buffet me up to cause me to present myself with sin, but it was the man, Jesus Christ, that lifted up and rose and snatched the thorn out of my flesh just as He took the keys of life and death when He went to hell. Oh, I went to hell will Jesus Christ with my weakness. I was made strong. Jesus's grace was sufficient in my weakness. I couldn't speak to anyone, not even the pastor who shepherds the sheep of the pasture because they would have discredited me and say it was me. No one could tell me how to move this out of my flesh until I resurrected with Jesus Christ.

Written by Melanie Hightower

The Testimony of
"The Thorn in My Flesh"

It was a season in my life. I didn't know why I kept going back to drugs, but I was listening to Noel Jones's teaching, and he brought out a point in his lesson and the word, and just then I understood it was Satan, the sin in me, and I understood why God allowed the thorn to stay there because I was high lifted and thought I was better than others because of the many gifts I was blessed with. I could sing, dance, speak, write portal, and teach very buff up, so God had to bring me down to let me see it was Him that was perfect, and all knowledge belong to Him.

Who Was the Woman of Wisdom?

Was she the woman who was seen in the Garden of Adam and Eve? Was it Eve's wisdom of Solomon that she conceived?

Or was she the wisdom of God that spoke everything in existence that called everything into their perfect places the moon and the stars?

Or was it her from the Garden of Adam and Eve who gave birth to Jezebel, the wicked queen who conceived that evil king, the seed of Adam who ate the forbidden fruit that Eve gave to him the tree of knowledge of good and evil.

Who were the women of wisdom?

Written by Melanie Hightower

The Testimony of
"The Woman of Wisdom"

I wrote this poem based on the fact when I first got introduced to rock cocaine. After taking the first hit, it opened my mind. I was able to feel good or evil. The word of God was in me since birth, and before I was baptized with the Holy Spirit, God allowed what the devil meant for evil. God used it for good. But through my addiction, addicts have crafty behavior.

God used cocaine to fashion my heart, which cocaine was a weapon of Satan. The word would spring up in me, which would be the Holy Spirit leading me in the path of righteousness. It speaks, tried the spirit by the word of God and tried the word by the Spirit. The spirit of wickedness will try and have me do deceitful thing to get money to support my habit. This was wicked knowledge such as wisdom like committing fraud, pickpocket, but the word of God kept me, and the word of God said acknowledge Him in all your ways, and He will direct your path, but I was a close-minded child and gullible. God used what the devil meant for evil for His good. So who was wisdom? God called wisdom she, and to me wisdom is given through women.

Proverb 1:20 states, "Wisdom crieth without she uttereth her voice in the streets." Women can teach their children wrong ways to gain in life just as Jacob in the Bible. His mother helped him trick Esau out of his birthrights. So I took the good from that old forbidden fruit tree, rock cocaine.

Press

The pressure of life engulfed me all through the years. I shared many tears. Life does has its up and downs, but "oh" how sweet the memories of yesterdays sound, but it was the sadness of yesterdays that played a major part. It was the seasoning of my growth that enabled me to go, but when I thought I made it to the finish line on December 31, I laid down my crown, but I didn't see heaven or a crown. Then I heard a voice so sweetly sound said, "Child of little of faith, take hold until you complete this race. You must not rest until you experience the resurrection of My death. I took hold of you so I could see you through forgetting those things, which are behind, press and hold on to faith." Christ, you will see at the end of the race.

Written by Melanie Hightower

The Testimony of "Press"

I went to a drug rehab, and I stayed focus on the months and years. I stayed sober. That was my goal. I strived for each month and year. I stayed clean. Eventually I knew I was going to relapse because that was my motive and to outdo others. At the end of each year, I want life to end because like I said, I knew I was going to relapse until the revelation of Christ spoke to me and told me I had to experience His death on the cross, and I did eventually I was crucified by people humanity, insults misjudge, and falsely accused.

Strange Path

A strange path was strange to me, so I asked the Lord if He would please reveal Himself to me. He touched me with a ray of sunlight.

That's when I began to see it was Jesus clothing me at Calvary cross
     where I first was lost.
A helmet of salvation, he said to me to renew my way of thinking
     that's why this path was strange to thee.
Breastplate of righteousness to protect thee from Satan's evil devices
     girded with the truth. I will always be with you, a stranger to
     this path you would no longer be.
Shod your feet with the gospel of peace and watch demons flee.
Now I see this strange path was just the renewing of me.

Written by Melanie Hightower

The Testimony of "Strange Path"

This is a point in my life that the filthy garments was stripe, and I was reclothed. God put the full armor of Him on me, and I was truly reborn again, not by my own strength because my own strength was principal of drug rehab, but it was done by the hands of God. That's why it was strange to me. It was supernatural by God's hands, and no rehab are by some minister could say it was their organization that did it by their standards. "Let the Redeemer of the Lord say so." Amen.

I Won't Complain

How could I complain about anything when my birth line and destiny isn't mine? Even when failure came, it was just a lesson to learn, and learning was my stepping stone, even when the stone was thrown in a blazing fire. Oh my god, how high I jumped up to reach the sky because Satan was dumb when he threw the stones in the fire to burn my feet to slow me down. Didn't he know I could reach the sky to my heavenly Father with a shout out loud, "Lord, have mercy!" I can't, and I won't complain.

Even if my bloodline stays the same, I won't die because I won't complain. The desert was hot, the rain poured and cried with thunder, but still I won't complain. Laid in the streets of Downtown LA, Skid Row, like a beggar man, but God has given me hope and a new name. I've learned how to bore pain, not hurting others, learning to give a helping hand. No, I won't complain. No, I won't. I will not judge even when I've been your rug, stepping all over me and on me. No, I won't complain. I learned the great humility of a servant. I did gain wealth and fame. Wealth of love, fame, or goodness, I won't complain. That's Jesus's way, nail to the cross. He defeated Satan without complaining and took His suffering and gain by not complaining.

Written by Melanie Hightower

The Testimony of the Poem
"I Won't Complain"

I wrote this poem, which inspired me to write. This poem was the fact I learned whatever stage I am in, in life, God sees you, and He knows that your true enemy is Satan, and he is the accuser who accuse God's people day and night. God tells us it is better to have a little than the abundance of the wicked, and most of God's prophets suffered much. They were not in fine clothes, so my experience living in Skid Row, Los Angeles, caused me to fall so deeply in love with Christ because of the people He sent my way. I will not or won't let Satan tempt me to do anything wrong to gain my needs or wants. I trust God today, so I won't complain.

Project Star

Enter into my heart from the very start "A Project Star," a fallen star broken in pieces, shattered dreams everywhere, and was spilled on dry land. But *often wondered why this fallen project star became the subject of my heart and mind. I knelt down to pick up the pieces. I tried to get a glimpse of his face that I could trace through time and space. "Wanted" in the want ads, I spelled out his name. Suddenly the mail carrier came. There it was from this project star that became the subject of my heart and mind. Now I could see this project star was birth in the inward part of me, blankets of love that burst through eternity into time for a new beginning for all those to see this project star of mine was just the subject of my heart and mind.*

Written by Melanie Hightower

The Testimony of "Project Star"

This particular time in my life, I met a guy, and I then I knew after our meeting that he was an angel that came to protect me. Never once did he speak or talk to me, he sat in my tent and said not a word. I tried to speak to him by questioning him, but he would not speak. He knew I wanted to ask him if he was an angel, but I know righteous angels don't make themselves known. It was on a night, and the street of Los Angeles was very dark on a full moon, but his presence comforted me. But as I remember, I felt peace in his presence, and he left just before daybreak. In my mind, I thought he would become my boyfriend, but the message came later that he was an angel.

Letters to the Churches

Have you heard or read the seven letters to church? Repent or else you would lose your lampstand? It would be removed by God. He said He would come quickly if you don't repent. Don't you know you need your lamp to see with your spiritual beams (eyes) that Jesus is your light? God need to see Jesus Christ, His Son, inside of you. There is no more sacrifice of blood of the lamb on your doorpost, so when the death angel row in, he has to see Jesus Christ.

Repent churches of Ephesus. God knows your works and how you labor and thy patience and how thou canst not bear them, which are evil, and thou has tried them, which say they are apostles and are not and found them to be liars. Yeah, we know. God knows you did labor, but you shall not escape the death angel unless you repent. You left your first love, Jesus Christ. Don't you know your work are dead without love of the center man that isn't dead? Jesus Christ, who God from above gave His only begotten Son. Yeah, you hated the practice of the Nicolaitans, so did God, but repent here. What the spirit is saying to you is if you have an ear, then hear, "Oh, Smyrna, how did you get trapped in the synagogue of Satan? Come out and repent."

This is what the letter to the angel of the church said, "Return unto Jesus, or else you're light of Jesus Christ would be removed. God knew your poverty that you are not rich. Come out quickly, or else God would come quickly to remove your lampstand." Mercy and grace were the letters to the church given to you. It is a chance to return unto Him who holds life and death in His hands. To the church in Sardis, he who has the seven spirits, God has not found your works perfect, and you have a name among the people that you are not dead but is alive in false fame who then blames you, so repent, or else God would come quickly to remove your lampstand.

If thou don't, you would not know the hour or time God would come upon thee. He will come like a theft in the night. Yeah, and no one knows the hour of a theft or the time. You know I am right.

Oh, churches in Philadelphia, how awesome are you that God has set before thee an open door no man can shut. You have little of strength, but you have kept God's name and His word, but there is one thing I know to be true, you have not denied God's name. So therefore, God said He would make them of Satan's synagogue, which they say they are Jews and are not, but they did lie. Yeah, churches in Philadelphia, you are favored by God and said He will make them of Satan's synagogue. Come and worship before thy feet, and they would know God has love thee. These are the Basis-Instruction-Before-Leaving-Earth. Repent before your lampstand be removed.

Written by Melanie Hightower

The Testimony to the Poem "Letters to the Churches"

I was inspired to write this poem being that I was knowledgeable of God's ways. When He brings a warning to you in your heart and spirit and you don't take heed, the removing of your lampstand is death. That is what brought me in. God chases who He loves, but he would cause sickness as well to get your attention. He threw Jonah in the belly of a whale, but God knew I feared him. I would obey. These letters were people who God knew. They fell by the wayside, but some of them did have some good works. God used me in dark places even in my drug addiction. It was many I ministered to.

Atiya

Atiya is a child that I birthed for a nation to reach many. It was a special plan that I didn't seek God or even have on my agenda. She was a child that I thought I would rearrange into the woman I long to be way before she was ever conceived by me. "Atiya," which is Arabic, spoke through me and gave me the meaning of her name, which means "gift," She was six pounds and nine ounces.

I kept Atiya close by my side, but blinded by the feeling of defeat, the chief of darkness spoke through the judge, and she was taken from me. Birth before pain, the book of Jeramiah explained Racheal weeping for her children spoke loud and clear and said to me the land became desolated because there were no more children.

The archangel spoke and said to me, "Trials and tribulation are your contractions. Push!" The saints said to me, "Watch how God brings thou children back to thee. Every race, nation, color, and creed will see how I brought thou children back to thee."

I have given you a new name "Athalia." God shall be exalt.

Written by Melanie Hightower

The Testimony of "Atiya"

Atiya was a child that I didn't plan. I was married, but my husband was incarcerated, and I relapsed on drugs, and I meet a guy that offered me to smoke with him. I accepted the offer, not knowing he was going to force me to have sex with him, but he did, and I conceived Atiya. I didn't believe in having an abortion. I knew God, but I didn't understand what God was doing. I was married and didn't have kids for my husband. So Atiya was born, and obviously God had a purpose because only God can allow pregnancy.

While I was carry Atiya, I was looking in the book of names to name children, and I saw the name *Athalia* and saw the meaning, which means "God shall be exalt." I asked my sister what she thought, and she looked over some names and said I should name her Atiya. The meaning of Atiya was "gift." Now you can see it was all in God's plan to give me the name *Athalia*, not my daughter. Atiya was a child God used to break the curse that was going on in my bloodline for decades over sexual heated that spirit lasciviousness. Only I can relate because the night I conceived Atiya, the spirit of lasciviousness was in the midst of conceiving her. I was going through menopause, and I couldn't conceive anymore children, but in some cases, a woman can conceive during menopause, and I did, so Atiya was a gift, even though I had her from another man, but I was tricked into having sex with him.

Atiya was born, but later she was taken, and then later she was adopted illegally. Atiya later found her grandmother, and through her grandmother, we came back together. I struggled with Atiya's emotion about how and why she was adopted. I had to fight with the lies that was told to her. It was painful for me because of the things she would say to hurt me. She didn't want to except me as her mother, but God told me He would heal her, and it would be a perfect bond from my womb. The truth would be revealed by God Himself. God has been exalted by the writing of this book with the new name He has given me "Athalia" because He did bring all my children back to me, and it will be some that will be birthed in the reading of these poems.

I have been insulted by family members being that I was the one always praising God but constantly falling some of the lies, and negative seeds were planted in Atiya from one of my sons and family members as well, but it was time I got the chance to minister to Atiya, and I will tell her how it is important for her to keep her virginity until marriage and don't be flattered by boys who would flirt with her because the word of God tells us beauty is passing, and charm is deceit, but a woman of God shall be praise.

I say to boys, girls, women, and men that flirtatious is deceitful, but my desire for Atiya is to not let the curse of lasciviousness continue. I celebrate today that I don't desire sex. I am standing in the gap for my children because we all should know this spirit lasciviousness can't enter into the new Jerusalem or the kingdom of heaven. There were times Atiya would reject me, but I would tell her if all I would do is just plant a seed from the word of God, I have done my purpose, and God shall be exalted.

BOOK 2

Confession of a Poet

Chapter 1

THE HOMECOMING

I grew up with a mother of three daughters: Tammy Goodall, who is resting in peace, Robin Goodall, and me, Melanie Hightower. My mother was married to Robert James Goodall, who is resting in peace. My mother is a very sweet mother and a sweet person. I believe my mother was called to be married only to God Himself, but she got married to my father and was told because her mother and father were strict, and she wanted to leave their household, so she got married to my father and had children. She got pregnant after marriage. A married woman seeks to please her husband, but an unmarried woman seeks to please God, which I struggled until God perfected me in showing me why He was searching through our bloodline for a woman only to be married unto Him.

Back then, they were called nun, but now we use the word *celibate*, which we often, some of us, misplace the word *celibate* by saying we are celibate because we separated from our husbands or have not yet married, but a celibate woman is married to God Himself that don't desire sex. Period. Well, she did good by directing us to God, by showing us Christ in her, in showing and taking us to church every Sunday and Sunday school.

The love my mother gave us wasn't spoiled love, it was just as the women of Jerusalem who God gave the best of everything, but one thing about it Is God doesn't make mistakes. God still had a plan for our bloodline; He didn't give up my mother. —— has lots of wisdom of God, and she didn't cast her wisdom to just anyone. I've learned wisdom to cry out loud to those that will hear her and, boy, did she "girl that boy no good" and so on.

Well, I was told I was a baby when my father went to prison, so I did not meet him until I was about eight years of age. I had grandparents who would say bad things about him and us such as, "You're just like your daddy," but how could that be when my mother was a perfect example of love? We had an auntie who loved us as well as my mother. My grandparents were very strict on us. I believe, because of my father's attributes, they wanted to make sure we didn't turn out to be like him, but hey, we were his seeds. Nothing could change that only through Christ Himself, which God did for me.

I chose to walk with my mother shoes and serve. God blesses, not curses. I was a child that was stuck with playing with dolls way over the age a child should have overgrown, but back as I could remember, God has chosen me then. I wanted a family with children and raise my children to learn how to communicate with me as their mother not with spanking. Never did I think of a father while playing with these dolls. I was the head as I saw my mother as the head, but as I grew up, we were labeled as dysfunctional because my father was not there, but I learned those were lies from the pits of hell.

God was the head of my mother, even though my father was not there. My mother love Christ even till this day. She never once miss church, and I could never remember her getting sick. She always worked. I never forget how she cleaned rich white people's house to support us and always was giving to the church. She always got us up for school and fixed breakfast for us and iron our clothes. You would never suspect we were poor.

I was the youngest, and my mother made sure my other sister knew I was the baby, and she taught them to have patient with me by me being the youngest. I remember we were playing a game call jacks, and I would miss the ball the very first try, and my mother would be in the kitchen cooking, and she would hear my sister telling me I missed, and when it was the next sister's turn, my mother would say, "No, give her another chance," and still today I am their baby sister.

I have one sister who would protect me, at least tried to, when my mother would chastise me with a spanking, she will yell and tell my mother not to hit me. Well, this particular day, my father was getting out of prison, and I was happy because I was finally getting to meet him. My father walked in the house with my mother, and I ran and yelled Daddy and jumped in his arms. My sister, who was next to me, said, "That's not your daddy." I don't recall if he heard her, but something struck in me, but it was strange. She was his favorite.

My father, a spiritual man, knew I was chosen for Christ. He would call me dumb. He made fun of the way I was holding my fork. He always found fault in me, giving him a reason to yell at me. He had an angry attitude toward me all the time, but God knew I needed everything I got from my mother before he got out of prison and came home. He, for some reason, could not tear myself esteem down because the heart I had was chosen for Christ.

I don't know if I was weaned from my mother, but Satan was defeated because my mother would rebuke my father when he would yell at me out of anger. The enemy would use my sister, who I was next, to get my father to yell at me. She would go tell my mother everything I was doing wrong to get my father to yell at me, but today I made it.

Chapter 2

SHAME

I went to a school named Carnegie Junior High in Carson, California, and my mother was divorced from my father at this time of my life. As I recall, it was girls my age that was dating guys. I always thought that I was ugly because guys didn't try and get at me, but they knew I was a nerd, and I was not easy. I talked to myself such as pretending, which these days they call it a mental problem, an imaginary friend.

My sisters didn't really school me about anything an older sister should have done since my mother had lots on her plate. Well, I was in the sixth grade and went to Carnegie Junior High School in Carson. I loved playing with my neighborhood friends. I remember they got bicycles to ride to school because school was a long way to walk. I had to get up early to get to school on time, so in that particular day, I had to walk alone.

After school, I came home and asked my mother to buy me a bike. She said no, and I made an outburst toward her and became stubborn. I didn't want to eat dinner as if to hurt my mother. Finally I gave in because I got hungry. Well, I went to school the next day, which I had to walk alone. When I made it home after school, I walked in the house, and my mother said to me, "Since you acted so ugly yesterday, go in the garage and get the clothes out of the dryer and fold and put them all up."

I dropped my books right by the door and pushed door open to the garage, and there it was a purple ten-speed bicycle. My mother understood that I wanted to ride to school with my neighborhood friends. She was such a understanding and loving mother. I never missed having a father. I never used that as an excuse for my addiction on drugs. I will explain further in this book.

Well, before I got this bicycle, I met a guy who was in one of my class, and he offered to walk me home. I was shock because he was the most popular guy in the whole school because he was handsome, but we used the word *fine* and being that I knew I was a nerd and didn't understand how he would be attracted to a person like me, but a plan and a plot of Satan, he had to start his mission early on me to stop the assignment of Christ. My purpose, his purpose, was to defile my body, body of Christ. So I accepted his offer, and he walked me home.

When we arrived to my house, I told him to wait at the door while I go and put my books up. When I got to my room and lay my books on the dresser, I turned around, and there he was behind me. He pushed me to my bed and tried to get on top of me. I push him off me real hard and told him out of a holy argue, "Get out!" It had to be God. He ran out. Well, I was embarrassed, and there was no one in my room or at home. Why did I feel embarrass? Maybe it was because I allowed him to walk me home. I felt as though I was wrong by accepting his offer, and I also was embarrassed because he desired me sexually, not as the girl I was.

God ordained me in my mother's womb because of what was in my heart to know marriage before sex and mainly a man should look at a woman by inward beauty and character. Well, I pretended to be sick and told my mother I didn't feel good. She agreed for me not to go to school, and I didn't. The guy caused myself esteem to drop, and part of my childhood happiness decreased because Satan used him to attack my self-esteem first, and being the age I was, I felt I disappointed of God.

This guy had the nerve to appear at my door. He rang the doorbell, and I answered the door. It was him. He asked me why I didn't come to school. I immediately told him to leave and don't come back, and I slammed the door.

The next day, I went to school, and my mother felt as though I was okay even though I knew I was never sick, and I could not convince her. I still felt sick. I never told anyone about what this boy did to me. I just allowed it to tear my value and worth down, selfesteem. Well, after getting to class, I saw him and still felt embarrassed, but I looked back. It had to be holy argue that kept my composure when it came to face him head-on. He had put a note on my desk. I picked it up to read. After sitting down, I read it and wrote in big letters *bug off* and throw it back on his desk. I noticed after I did that, some of the boys in class ran up to his desk to see what I wrote back to him, and that day I knew they had sided with each other to see if they could get me to have sex. This took a lot out of my self-esteem.

When I got into high school, I walked the halls going to and from classes with my books held close to my chest. My self-esteem was stripped. Now I had a sister who we were a year apart. I wanted to stick close to her, but she would ditch me. Being I was younger than her and a nerd, she did not want anyone to know I was her sister. Well, I later discovered I had big brothers in high school that knew my character because of the Christ in them. It was the intervention of Christ that showed me who they were. They would joke with me and let me hit them in their heads with my paper folder, but after class, they would go their way somehow.

They knew I was a virgin. Boy, did I enjoy their company. Before class would start, they helped my character to come out. Now I didn't know about being a woman, that we would have a monthly period, which is called menstruation. The last bell rang for school to be over. I was in high school at this time in the eleventh grade, and my menstruation started. I thought I had to urine, so I hurried to the restroom so I would not urinate on myself and would not miss the bus to take me home. I rushed to the restroom and pulled down my pants, and I saw blood. I started my menstruation, but I didn't know what it was. I quickly pulled up my pants and ran out and jumped on school bus in time.

I went home and got there and showed my next to the oldest sister. She laughed and said, "You just started your menstruation." She gave me a tampon. It is what women use to protect their underclothes, but she should have started me with pads.

Well, the high school prom came about. I was in the twelve grade, getting ready to graduate from high school. I didn't have a date who wanted a nerd. Well, my mother's best friend's son ended up taking me to my school prom. I still was a nerd, but eventually I started going through the way of the generation in my days, having boyfriends and having sex. The first time I went to bed with a guy who I met on my first job, I was seventeen years old.

After graduation from high school, I still had low self-esteem. Haven't I known this guy thought I was loose, I probably would not have accepted a date with him, but after that experience with the guy in junior high school, I dealt with low-self-esteem, and any guy that would make me feel attractive, I would compromise with them.

Well, he picked me up, and after dinner, we went to a place where he worked, which was a house they were building, and he did security work there until the house was completed. His plans were to have sex with me, but I didn't know because of wanting to be liked by someone. We began to have sex, and when he went into me, he discovered I was a virgin. He did ask me. Now that I remember I told him no, not knowing men could tell once they go into a female if they were a virgin or not. Well, he did, but he didn't want to break my virginity. He came out of me and said, "I thought you said you were not a virgin. Put your clothes on."

I thank God he didn't because later on in life, when my virginity got broken, I discovered that was a lot of pain. I believe God told him not to, or he was a gentleman. Still I felt shame because I felt as though he thought I was weak, which the devil caused me to have shame. Well, my father raped me, and when he did, I guess he noticed I was a virgin and came out of me. I don't know if he spewed in me, but I ran to my oldest sister's house and told her. I showered and took a female douche, which they could not prove because I did that.

Chapter 3

LOOKING FOR MY TRUE IDENTITY

I ended up losing my first job and getting turn out on drugs. Searching for my true identity, I did seek to higher education by going to college but didn't know what I really wanted to do in life. God knew He was going to allow me to go through a lot of stages of life to bring me back to that person He designed my heart to be as that person. I was in junior high school when I knew a female was not supposed to exchange her body for really false love sex before marriage, which is not ordain by God. This was Satan's biggest weapon to use on mother's daughters, whose mother was raising daughters on her own and never do the mothers think of the importance of telling her daughter the facts of life from God being there only worry is to provide food and clothes for them.

Well, my oldest sister didn't seem to struggle with giving her virginity away so easily or even struggle with self-esteem, and some girls feel it's called maturity to deal with it or outsmart the guy, but not when you are chosen by God. God knew He would be my father and raised me. Now I do believe a man should raise their daughters, and a mother should raise their sons.

I attended Long Beach City College in Lakewood, California, and I studied theatrical dancing, being that that spirit entered in my mind, my outward beauty is what's going to give me a career. Well, I had to still have the base subjects such as English, math, and so on once you enter college as well, and this one particular night, which was an English class if I can remember, I didn't study, and I asked my sister to go to my night class with me to help me cheat on a test. She agreed if I would take her to a bar to meet up with her boyfriend after my class was over. I agreed.

Well, after class, I did just that. She wanted me to wait in my car to go see first if her boyfriend was there, and being that I wasn't twenty one, I could not go in with her anyway, and you had to have proof of your age. Well, she was taking too long to come back out to tell me if she was going to stay or if her boyfriend was there. Being I was tired, I got out of the car and locked the doors, and I went to see what was taking her for so long. I got to the door, and the security stopped me and asked me to present some identification to him to show proof I was twenty-one years old. Well, I didn't have proof, and I kept trying to convince him I was twenty-one years of age, and there was this guy behind me and said, "She is twenty-one. I have known her for twenty-one years." I turned around to see who this guy was, knowing I wasn't twenty-one years old.

When I turned around, he said to me, "What is wrong? You can't get in the club."

I said no. He asked me to step aside and let him talk to me. I did being he was very fine, long hair, and all a trick of Satan's outward looks that had my mind to seek after in men as well same spirit. Satan came after me in junior high school with the finest guy on campus. Well, I fell for Satan's trap again. I came to find out this guy was a pimp, and I never thought that was a reality. I thought pimps just played in movies. Well, he ended up kidnapping me and drove me to Hollywood to a motel, and there at the motel, he had a girl there, that later I discovered, she was his girlfriend from high school. He had her tell me how to work the streets.

Now when she told me to charge the guys $25.00 for sex, I looked at her if she was crazy. The first day she took me to the streets to prostitute, we both got in a car with this guy who wanted both of us. We went to a motel with him. He came up to me as if to touch my breast and asked me to take off my clothes. I grabbed a lamp to hit him and told the girl I was with to run. I grabbed his pant, and we run out of the room with his pants and wallet. I could not see myself selling my body for $25.00. I'm worth more value than $25.00 dollars.

Well, I know you are wondering why I didn't call police or get help from this pimp. At this point in my life, I had very low self-esteem, and the thought of dressing up, looking glamourous excited me, and I was struggling in college. So I dealt with this pimp for just a season of my life, and I had problems with giving him money that I sold my body for. I ran away from him and became a prostitute, but I was not on drugs such as hard drugs, but I smoked weed. Now I still had my virginity because I never had sex with them. God had a plan, and he protected my virginity by moving it out of the way supernatural (huh).

God is awesome and all-powerful. I was what you call a happy hooker. Well, my oldest sister turned me out on rock cocaine, and I became addictive to it because I liked it. I began working in the streets to support the habit. It medicates my pain, and it took me in a world that was not real, but it made me feel like I was a queen.

I meet a guy who I fell in love with, which was false love as well. He was abusive, but he had his own place, and he got high too. I work to support our habit because he was get help from the governor to pay our rent, but he would do some strange things to me that I won't mention in this book.

I got further and further from the person I was, but God is a one-time God. The lessons I've learn I would not change for nothing, and I don't regret nothing I've been through. I am stronger and wiser. Well, this guy who I was with. We were having sex, and it became real painful for me. It felt as though he was knocking against something in me. He was breaking my virginity, but I didn't know, so I put my nails in his side real hard to get him to get off me.

I was about twenty-one years old. He jumped up off me and was laughing. I grabbed my clothes and put them on and ran to my sister's house around the corner and told her what happened. She laughed as well and said he bust your cherry, meaning virginity. I would not believe her, so she took me to the hospital, and it took the doctor to explain it to me. Well, I returned back to this guy, still not knowing who I was, doing drugs, allowing this guy to abuse me, and so on. I finally left him for good.

The word tells us in the last days wicked men are going to go into gullible women's household who is loaded up with every sin and tear these women's household down. God said these women were forever learning, but they would not acknowledge the truth. Well, I finally did, but I continued to work the streets and use drugs. God started to bring men in my life that would protect me. We would come with tricks, but I started to acknowledge God in all my ways of walking. He said He would direct our path, and God did, but God had to really teach me as a woman, and He did no matter how my mother was wondering why I turned the way I was. God had a plan way before I was born.

Now in the book of Jerimiah, God spoke to the prophet and told him to go to Jerusalem and speak to her about her ways. God gave this woman everything that was the best, but she gave it to her lovers what God gave her, and she bore children unto these men of different nationality. She was an outcast, but God built her up and caused her to become very beautiful, and because of her beauty, her name went through the land, which was fame, but God called her weak because she did not cause these men to marry her. Now when I became knowledgeable of this, when I read it, I couldn't relate to really what God was saying because I did not like giving my money to no man, but in that book of Jerimiah 16, God did tell the prophet to tell Jerusalem that even prostitutes get paid, but she was paying all her lovers, but in that chapter, I saw how God was sending men to give to me without asking for sex.

At this point, I was really abusing drugs. There were days I wasn't able to get a motel to stay in. I couldn't come up with money to pay for my room for that day because of my drug using. But I still didn't understand God's message to me in that chapter because I became a prostitute, but later in life, God chose me to be New Jerusalem, where He said there would be no dogs, thieves, fornication, and lasciviousness can't enter, and He was getting me to the point I hated all those things over sexually heated men, which is what lasciviousness is, and dogs are male prostitutes, and that is what these man I was fallen in love with. They made women feel as though they loved them by making them feel good in the bed, but they really were selling themselves to women so the women could take care of them. This is what the New Jerusalem is going to be like because of what the old Jerusalem did.

I suffered doing correction, but it brought me back to who I was in. Here God judges the heart, these wicked angels built their character in me, which became strongholds, and I was blind by those strongholds, but my heart stayed still. I became really hard on men. They had to meet my standard or hit the road.

At this point, I didn't feel sorry for men, not even a bomb on the streets, not even a begging man. I probably hated men, but I was not gay, which was not right. If you read my book *Testimony of a Poet*, you would see how God brought me out, giving me the gift of love. I still was searching for my true identity when it was right in my heart. I have should have been the person that was in my heart no matter what others were doing, but I paid a price for the person I was. The battle was rough, but it was worth a fight. I took back what Satan stole from me. I was looking for my true identity in the street's life. But it came through the redeemer of the Lord who raised me to be the women I am today.

Chapter 4

SEARCHING FOR MY IDENTITY

I continue to work the streets and use drugs, and I became very angry against men who looked for women to score payment for sex. I felt they should have compassion for the women who were on drugs, prostitute for their habit, being that God created men and women, the weaker vessel, but I didn't know these wicked angels came in the form of men, which they used them to connect to the flesh of another.

The spirit of lasciviousness was like a germ; it needed a body to live. God didn't take it lightly about this unclean spirit, even though Paul said to marry if the couple who are engaged in a relationship can't estrange their flesh from sex, marry so the women's bed won't burn in lust, but for the women, God chose to sanctify. There is no excuse with God, but the word tell us many are called, but few are chosen.

When you call a person, it doesn't mean they would answers a person that is chosen. God chose them in their heart. No matter how hard you try to act out of the heart, it won't work. You won't feel comfortable doing whatever it is you are acting out of. What is in the heart overpower anything. So I began to really come down on the men that would pick me up. I didn't care if I stole their money and so on. I just felt they all should have just given it to me because I was a woman in distress and the weaker vessel, but Satan had his assignment as well. He was out to win my soul. He knew who I was and my chosen purpose. He hated me as well, and he used men to manifest his hate toward me.

I was picked up by a white men at knifepoint. He raped me, and he was driving at one point to go to this area called Signal Hill, and the Spirit said he was going to kill me. I immediate took both of his hands off the steering wheel, and at that time, he was going through intersection, and he stopped somehow and yelled at me to get out. I was butt naked. I know you wondering how I ended up with my clothes off with him, just having a knife, but fear crimped me. I couldn't think until the Holy Spirit revealed he was going to kill me.

When I jumped out of the car, there were this police on his way to work. He did not have his uniform on because they should be in uniform when they get to work. He saw me get out of the car screaming. He jumped out of his car and put his shirt around me. I noticed his badge on his shirt. He calmed me down and took me to the Signal Hill Police Station, but the guy got away. Satan really wanted to kill me. He knew at that point I was going to defeat him and his angels. I started revealing to these men who I was and how I got addictive to drugs.

I didn't care about any man on the streets, but I met one guy who I believe he cared about me. I would set the men up to be robbed by him. He felt the way I did about men picking up women for sex, but there is one thing he said to me, and that was he was my guardian angel, but I knew at this point and time in life, angels don't reveal themselves.

He gave me a book written by a Jehovah witness. The book brought knowledge to me about these disobedient angels who left their position and looked at beautiful women and went to bed with them, and these women bore children unto them and how God destroyed that generation and chained those angels in darkness. God still used him for His glory, though, I believe he was a ruler in darkness. He did protect me. I fell in love with him, and at that point, I believe God wanted to bring me and him out of darkness together to testify about Satan and his angels on how we went through.

I started minister to the people on rock cocaine as well as using with them, but the spirit of God would take control. I will tell them, "Greater is he that is in us than he of the world." Some would receive what I was saying, and some wouldn't because I was using. I started searching for who I was to Christ, and the battle got tough. I was led back to my heart, and I knew I was a women that was supposed to be well respected because I was a women.

I found myself through the relationship of this guy I was in love with. He knew my character, and he suffered with me on the streets. I would ask him to go to church with me, and he would tell me without words being spoken he could not go into the church. I will hear his spirit speak and tell me this. I recognized he either had to be a ruler in dark places. I know in the word God gave me, it said he told Michael to watch His people until He returns, so I went on to continue in this relationship. I remember asking him to go and buy me something to wear. I wanted to see how he looked at me as a woman. He brought an outfit that was modest. He would tell me not to go out and prostitute, but I was hooked on drugs, and I didn't understand how the spirit of Christ would use me on drugs, and God did not deliver me.

This went on about ten years. I got pregnant with my second child, and it was not his baby, which I thought it was. I had a baby boy, and I called him Dashawn. After I gave birth, I went to a rehab and got him out of the system at the age three because there were drugs found in his system. Well, this rehab was a Christian rehab, and the format was the word of God. There was a woman pastor who was the founder, a very beautiful women who I kept my eyes on. I never would forget how she worn this light-blue robe with a white dove.

At the end of it was the beauty of Christ that I would see on her. She is what I desire to be a woman of God. I saw myself in her as though she carried me. Who knows? She properly birth me spiritually. There I was, baptized with the Holy Ghost, speaking in another language. I didn't have to search no more for my identity. The heart of my soul reign. I was taught to hold on my sobriety through going to Bible study and group meeting, which was principal because I was not yet delivered from rock cocaine. It became a struggle for me. When God delivers you, there is no struggle. God still had His plan because there is something God wanted to work through me and do, not people. My faith became in a program and not God and people. I was trusting people something God didn't like. The glory belonged to Christ.

I ended up relapsing because my faith was in the wrong people. I lost my son in the system again, but later I regained custody again. This became an ongoing thing. I started to serve God just to get my kids out of the system. This should have not been I found myself, but I didn't find God. I was not seeking Him with all my heart and soul, and He did not rest until I did, so I went through many stages in life until I sought God with all my heart, mind, and soul, and He was found.

I still struggle with self-esteem. I felt as though I wanted to share the beauty of Christ with someone, and I met a guy in the church rehab who, at first, told me he did not like me because he thought I was so holy. We fell in love, but the attitude I had against men I brought it into our relationship. I was very hard on him. He understood I was not having sex with him until we got married. He didn't have a job, and after group, we would go eat, and I would not pay for him, nothing to eat, because the word of God in the book of Jerimiah 16, it was always in my spirit and mind how God told Jerusalem the women He built up and gave the best of everything and she gave to men I didn't or won't to be that women he dealt with it.

Though, I got pregnant for him, but I lost the child. I was hurt, and I questioned God and asked Him why He allowed this to happen. He told me I could not conceive for these men. Satan and these disobedient angel followed me even in the church, but God had a plan. I understood God, but I don't know whether I wanted to receive that. I thought I was having a delusion in my mind, but it was so God wanted me to conceive a child to break this curse off me through a man that was a son of men and not a child of the sons of God, "angels." I finally received this spiritual seed from God, and as I write, I have to birth this message.

Chapter 5

STRUGGLE WITH GOD

I began to fight with God because I believe God was calling me to be a celebrity, and I thought it was Satan telling me these thing because in the church rehab, we study about how to notice and recognize false prophet, but it was God I was struggling with. I wanted to be married and raise a family with a godly man and have my kids godly, but God's plan was bigger than mine. I had to reach women who bore children unto these angels. That is why children get molested by parents on drugs, and some turn to homosexual because of these disobedient angels.

God didn't give up on me, and I don't regret anything I went through, even though people tried to make me feel as though I regretted everything I went through. I don't think so. I continued to struggle with God to release me from this purpose, but God chase who He chose for His purpose. I believe because I was bold like Esther in the Bible. Every relationship I got in God came in and caused havoc because He didn't want that for my life, and God knew Satan and His angels had to come to me with their best suits on to deceive me, which I kept putting what God was showing me in the back of my mind, but God would always come and stir me up when I would get comfortable in these relationships.

Every time I would try hard and get pregnant for the person I was in the relationship, it would not happen. I was getting in the way of God, even though He told me I could not bore for these men, and by all means, these were men I met in darkness. I have three children; they are eight years and nine years apart. Each child have a meaning to their name and purpose because of my rebelliousness. God allowed me to bore these three children, which I didn't plan, and I know it was God's doing because they are eight years and nine years apart.

The firstborn's name is Joshua, meaning salvation, and salvation means preservation or deliverance from harm, ruin, or loss and deliverance from sin and its consequences, so the birth of my son Joshua, God gave me salvation because I could have been destroyed from being disobedient unto God, but He knew I didn't understand my purpose just yet. My second son's name was supposed to Jehoshaphat, but I gave him that middle name, so his first name is Dashawn. God told me to name him Jehoshaphat, meaning never follow the ways of Balaam. It was a teaching where they taught its okay to fornicate and to eat things, sacrifice to idol gods, and now fornication was always okay in my bloodline. Parents still today don't really come on their children about marriage. God told me my son would never follow those ways. My third child was a girl. I named her Atiya, meaning gift. She was a gift to me.

I was overpowered by this guy I met doing drugs, and he wanted sex. I was afraid he would hurt me if I didn't, so I did, and I got pregnant for him. Well, I kept her because I did want another child but not that way. I said to myself I was going to raise her into the woman I longed to be and teach her to keep her virginity. God saw fit, though, Satan meant it to be evil. God still had a plan. I questioned God and asked Him why he allowed this to happen when I was married, and I didn't conceived for my husband.

This women came up to me at this sober-living home and asked to pray for my baby. She began to put her hands on my stomach and started speaking in tongues, and she said the Lord said, "It's a purpose." I knew she was sent by God because she didn't know I was married, and the baby I was carrying was not my husband's.

After that child, I didn't have any more children or conceive. So each child had a purpose in my life. I can truly say life is good with the teaching and learning experience with Christ. I could have died if it was not God on my side and had chosen me, but I continued to struggle with God about the nation Jerusalem, the weak women who were not a prostitute. God even admired a prostitute because a prostitute got paid, and she didn't give to her lovers what God gave her, so I didn't understand, even though I bore children out of marriage.

Who was I? It's the question I kept asking God as I speak. I remember my heart stood still. Satan could not allow anything to enter in my heart what God put in my heart. These other attributes were deceiving spirits, but could not deceive me because of my heart. I knew kings were born, and women could not build a king in men if they were not born to be a king like my son Jehoshaphat. He was a king. These sons of God tried to get me to invest money into them and build them as a king and sell drugs in the spiritual world. That's what the spirit would show me, and I knew this to be a false spirit. Some women on the streets did this, but Satan had a problem with me. I did blend in, and it was strange. Why did they take their attention off their women and chased me? It was Satan. He was angry I did not receive his false messages and teaching.

I separated from my husband, and he filed a devoice but never followed through with it. I didn't understand the purpose why we got married. I believe God used him to bring my self-esteem back. I was highly lifted, and my value and self-worth were manifested. We are still legally married, but I am no longer a women of adulteress. I don't desire sex. I became a woman living by the word of God, but there are things God still have to work out of for my spirit. I learned to be beautiful inward. Beauty is passing, and charm is deceit, but a woman of God shall be praised, so I learned that men that was of charm was deceitful, which was a late message, but God had His plan, and His plan always win.

After searching myself, I found out I had many talents. One was writing poetry and poems and mainly to be the mother God called me to be—loving, understanding, not argumentative, and accepting when I was wrong. I gained relationship with my children and got them out of the system, but that came later. I still struggled with drugs and God because of my drug addiction. I began going to jail and prison, and every time I got arrested, I would seek God by reading His word.

There was a scripture in the Bible where it spoke about he who walk among the seven stars speak to the angels at the church. Now God spoke through this scripture by telling me I walked among the seven stars because I would see the seven stars above my head no matter. If I went to the north side of town or the south or the east or west, those seven stars would be over my head. God was preparing me to be a prophetess, but I was not aware of it until he caused me to live in the book of Revelation to get the full birth of what he was saying. I lived in the house of Babylon house of demons in Downtown LA. Satan sent demons in the form of men to defile me with this sinful spirit lasciviousness.

Chapter 6

CHASTISED BY GOD

Well, I ended up on Skid Row, Downtown Los Angeles, California, using drugs every day, running from God, even though He knew where I was. If I made my bed in hell, He was there, but God was chastising me and trying to get my attention. He never gave up on me because He chose me. If it had not been me being fearful of God, where would I be? Fearful means you would reverence Him and His word. I finally did, but these demons in Babylon were powerful, but not as powerful as God.

There were big rats in downtown in Skid Row, and God used them to torment me. It is his way to chastise me so I would let these men come in my tent, thinking they would protect me from these rats. If I share my drugs with them, it didn't go that way being who was working behind Satan. How I would know is because I knew the word of God. They would ask me to have sex with them after me sharing with them. I would say no, and the word would spring up in me and say these might turn the grace of Jesus Christ to lasciviousness, and when the word would speak and tell me who they were, I would put them out of my tent, even though I was afraid of the rats.

There was this one guy who became a friend, but he seemed to be attractive to me and wanted me to be more than just a friend. He already had a girlfriend. We all became friends. She started to pick up that her boyfriend was attracted to me, and that became a problem, but I would tell men that I was not looking for a relationship. I was in a crisis, and I was not going to play house, and by all means, who wanted her boyfriend? He was an addict and had nothing to offer me.

Well, God chastise me by allowing me and his girlfriend to get in a physical fight. She hit me with a lock and broke my jaw because pride would not let me accept her trying to overpower me because of her jealousy. At this point in life, I didn't desire sex, and I began really crying out to God to deliver me. I wanted out of darkness, but I thank God there is light in darkness, Jesus. His word became a lamp unto my feet. Satan began to really fight me with every trick he had.

I didn't prostitute anymore. I became a panhandler begging for money to support my drug addiction. God is good. His people would buy me food, clothes, and give me money from five dollars to a hundred. I knew it was Christ that caused them to give to me. Jesus is love. God was forming my heart with love for His purpose.

I started loving men that they call bombs and begging men because Jesus had mercy for me. What made me think I was any different? Trust began to enter in me. See, Satan knew who I was. I didn't try to get over on people for my drugs. That's when I knew the desire was leaving me. I remember one time I asked this man for a cigarette, and he said he did not have anymore. He ask if he could trust me to go and buy a pack and come back because the restaurant he was at did not sell cigarette. I said yes. He passed me a hundred-dollar bill. I said to myself if he could just give me one dollar for going or one cigarette, I was going to still come back. See, Satan knew I was professing Christ and was supposed to live by the word. I outsmarted Satan and didn't allow the drugs to cause me to break the law because there would have been a consequence behind it, either death or I would have ended up in jail.

God broke the captivity off me. I no longer went to jail or prison anymore. Jesus said if we acknowledge Him in all our ways, He would direct our path, and I did for four years on the streets of Skid Row. I struggled with my addiction with love and kindness God drew me. I had everything I wanted and needed in my tent, and you properly couldn't tell I was homeless. It was God's grace and mercy that kept me and His chosen purpose for me. The one was this family that own a clothes store when I first ended up downtown. I didn't know about the mission or where to go to shower for homeless people. I was sitting on the sidewalk, and my monthly came on, and I didn't have a change of clothes. The Holy Spirit spoke and told me to go across the street and ask the people who own the store for a change of clothes and tell them my problem. I did as the Holy Spirit directed me to do, and they did as God lay on their heart to do as God directed them to do.

God has His people in secret places. These people became the source of my needs. Even through the chastising of Christ, God still provided for my needs. God doesn't pay evil for evil, even in our sins, He loves us. Nothing can separate the love of Christ from us. Now at this point, I wanted out from among Satan and his angels who were ruling the streets of Skid Row with drugs, immorality, fornication, and every wicked spirit in high places. There was this organization that was offering housing. I accepted the offer, and it seemed as though the filthy turban of wanting to use came off my head and the desire left me.

I ran to my tent to gather my things. Haven't I known that this girl was a drug demon. I would have left everything, but I didn't. When I got to my tent to pack up everything, she came running to my tent to ask me if I wanted a rug she didn't want, but prior to that, she already had asked me that, and I told her no before, and I told her again, but that was an excuse so she could enter into me again. This was what God was showing me about, Babylon, house of demons. Satan didn't care about exposing his imps boldly. He knew his time was short. God was going to defeat him through me. She stood in front of my tent as did a third-degree turn on the sidewalk, and then I felt her spirit get into me. I then I felt as though I wanted to use this since this is how God let me see the stronghold demon.

I then told myself I was not going anywhere with that demon. I was not going to enter the new with that drug demon, so I had to wait on God. So I declined to move. I said I was just going to stay in Babylon until God would deliver me. Well, I met this guy who would chase me all the time downtown. He would offer me money to go with him. He was handsome and had a lovely character.

Here goes Satan again in a form of a man. I was lonely and afraid of the rats, so one day I gave into his. Mind you, I didn't know this spirit lasciviousness became a stronghold, and this is something

God wanted to work out of me. This was the angel that bruised me with sons of God. The sex was good with this guy, and I know what the word Paul taught us and said if we could estrange our flesh, it's better to marry. I would always talk about marriage to him. He was crafty, he knew who I was, and he knew he couldn't marry me. His place was in darkness, the spirit who was standing up in him, the real men I didn't see because Satan stood tall in him.

If God wanted me and that man together, God had to deliver him as well because Satan had him and used him for a very long time. He believe his ways of thinking to lure women to be with him was right and the way to go. He was addictive to sex. I kept on denying the word of God. God was telling me through His word about these men who turned the grace of God to lasciviousness. I became like the sex with him as I was deceived to think I loved him, and I didn't I begin to hate that spirit lasciviousness. When he would come visit me, the first thing he would pull out of his pocket was cocaine and then start taking his clothes off. This is how God began to get my attention about who He was, and He didn't care if I would lose my soul. This spirit would take you to hell and then be destroyed in the lake of fire, the second death.

I fear God. I just didn't know how to come out, then later I learned I could not do it. It had to be God Himself to do it with His supernatural power, but God had to get me to hate the things He hated. When you begin to hate sin, God will deliver you out of all your troubles. The wretched woman that I was, who could have delivered me? No one but Jesus. Well, I did become to see Satan using this guy to try and steal my soul. I started refusing sex with him under the influence of drugs, and when he got an attitude and leave, it would be at night, and that was when the rats would come out and torment me, a part of God's chastisement and bad as I wanted him not to leave because I feared the rats. These rats also were Satan's weapon as well.

When God revealed that it was hell, I was in creeping creatures. God was telling me I was in hell facing death, and I would have to die in sin in darkness in hell. The second death would have to come, so even the beginning of knowledge is fear, so I wanted to show God

I hate drugs and sin by not given in to this guy. I let him leave. He did this for so long, which became a test. I became sick, and I didn't know I had kidney failure, but I knew my urine had a strange look to it, and my side inward would hurt me.

The word tells us in the book of Job God would get our attention one way or another in a deep vision of dream or in our bed of sickness to cause us to return to Him to keep us from going to the pits of hell, and God saw fit to do so because I kept compromise with sin.

I have a sister who lives in Long Beach, California, whose house I went to visit. I left her house that day to go to the emergency. I felt this was my chance to see what the problem was, so I left walking, which the hospital was a long way, but my intention was to beg for money and get something to smoke before I get to the hospital. God moved everything out of my way, and no one would give to me my son. I got tired, and there was a place on the side of the streets that had fresh grass, which looked good in my eyes, a place to rest. I lay down on the grass in the street from the hospital to rest. Before I went to set in emergency room, I went to sleep, and boy, was it a sweet rest.

I woke up and walked to the emergency room. They took my blood pressure, and the next thing I knew I was in intensive care. The nurses came everywhere, putting ice packs on me. I then asked what the problem was, and they said my blood pressure was high. I stayed in intensive care until it got low, then I was moved to another room. The nurse came and told me the doctor wanted to check my kidney and do a biopsy to see if my kidney was all right. Well, I left. I refused to stay. They made me sign paper, stating I was going against doctors' order. I went back to my sister's house, and there I began to tell her what the doctors wanted to do. I later said to myself that I better go and find out, so I went to St. Mary Hospital emergency and explain to them. I signed myself out of memorial hospital and what doctor said they did a follow-up and admitted me in hospital and come to find out I had kidney failure. God did get my attention.

Chapter 7

I WANTED TO DIE

Well, I stayed in hospital until they found me a place to stay because I let it be known I was homeless, and I need a dialysis center to accept me for treatment to clean my blood. Both kidneys were damage. It was taking a long time for them to do this, but they found a center to accept me for treatment, and my sister said I could live with her, so I left the hospital and moved in with my sister. I didn't understand the illness, and my family didn't either. They put a lot on me such as me having to clean up myself, and I was weak. The kidney caused men to look at the outward of me. I struggled with them trying to get them to understand. I didn't have the strength to do, so it became a problem.

I moved back with my mother, and at this time, our relationship was not right. My mother had anger and unforgiveness toward me, which caused strife between me and her. Mind you, I had unforgiveness toward her, but in reality, no one was ready for this illness I had. I believe it was more than just unforgiveness, it was the fear of me dying. They feared, and anger took place, which became a stronghold. My family didn't know how to love without gifts. Well, we had to learn, and that is what God had to do, but we had to be willing to let Him control by His word. We knew to go to church, but it was a form of godliness. We denied His power to help us through His word by obeying.

God's word is powerful, but God's purpose was to use my illness to do as well as healing me. At this point, we were a long way because we were comfortable in our abusive ways. We abused each other and didn't know how to confess when we were wrong because of pride, but being chosen, your heart is already fix in your mother's womb. Whether you are a male or female, if you choose your heart, your destiny is fixed. So I was willing, but before I got to this point, I wanted to die, and God knew I didn't fear death. If you hold on to your life, you would lose it, but if you let go of your life, you would gain it.

I was willing to accept my illness, and if God saw fit to end my life, I was ready. There were family members who spoke death over me tried to make me believe I was going to go to hell, but I would fight back them cursing me by telling them if God would send me to hell because of my addiction that I struggled with my own strength, then by all means, let His will be done because I didn't break God's law such as robbing and stealing for drugs. I didn't even prostitute anymore for drugs. I could not do what God had to do by His power. Rehabs were fighting by man's principal, and in my own strength and weak flesh, how could I? So I was ready to die.

My motherhood was taken most of my life. I used drugs. I felt I had no life, but God is life, and my life was not my own. I had to understand that. I remember it did on me in the hospital when my next to the oldest son came to visit me with my sister. It was put on my heart that I didn't fear death. I started crying, and they thought I was crying because my problem is death, but I was crying because I was going to leave them behind. That was an intervention with God.

They released me from the hospital, and like I said, I went to live with my sister, and guess what? Her boyfriend came and asked us if we wanted to smoke some crack cocaine. My sister looked at him, but she did not rebuke him for tempting me. I later discovered that was Satan's mission, to use them to tempt me and to set out again to destroy me. I was weak because, mind you, God had a plan. He knew I was not yet delivered from drugs by His hands. When God do it, it's done. No rehab, or you could get the credit. Let the redeemer of the Lord say so.

I began using heavy again, which I didn't let my mother know. My sister kept it sealed until she got mad at me and revealed it to my mother, which was mean because she allowed her boyfriend to do so. Mind you, she was using as well with speed, but they didn't know I was chosen, but they knew I was the only one really seeking Christ, so they had Satan's attributes, always accusing me night and day. Satan would use anyone who is not knowledgeable of your purpose, but the word tells us, if you cause someone to fall, it is better for a millstone to be tied around your neck and be throw in the sea. So I moved in with my mother, and I was sneaking to get high. They could not detect it, but God kept me being uncomfortable. It used to be fun, but God kept stirring me up. I couldn't sleep. I wasn't taking my medicines right.

I just wanted to die. I didn't have anything to live for. I got tired of fighting my drug addiction in my own strength. God had a plan, and by all means, I had to go through all these stages of life to accomplish his purpose, and that was to create the right spirit and a pure clean heart again by renewing me. I didn't care if I died like I said. God said no, so I continued feeling this way, me and the other reason. I wanted to die. There was no true love in my family. I found out love is not in giving. It is compassion, kindness, and understanding. It doesn't buff its own way, and it's long-suffering, willing one for another. It doesn't hold grudges. There are ways to show love in giving but not with the characters I just mention didn't go hand and hand with the giving.

I was tired, and I felt like I experienced what I believe is God's perfect peace. I went to sleep one evening, and boy, the sleep was so sweet and perfect to me I woke up and said, "Yes, Lord, I am ready. I want to rest now from this battle of drug addiction."

I met this girl downtown in Skid Row who became to like me, but the devil used her as well. Oh, I thought she was sent by God. She used God's name. She fed the homeless after she sold all what she was going to sell in her creole catering service. She would give the leftover to the homeless. Satan is very crafty. The word said he was craftier than any beast of the field. Well, I move in with her because I got tired of my family speaking death over me, and the girl I met downtown knew I used drugs. Her mother did as well, but she didn't. I had my own room, and there was this guy at the end of the alley of her house, who sold crack cocaine, but when I met her, she would speak of God, and I thought God would use her to fast and pray with me and kill the drug demon. "Huh," not so. I learned people hid behind God's name for self-gain.

God showed me who she was worshiping in her heart. She never went to church. She was an alcoholic, but I didn't judge her. Somehow I believed she was going to pray and fast with me. I told her how I wanted to give up drugs. The more I told her, the more she would offer me money to buy drugs. I thought maybe I should give her a hint. I would play my Christian music real loud all day, but she still did not get my message. I would take a video of a gossiping minister in her room, praising what they're teaching, but she still didn't get my hint. She continued to play world music and worship female and worldly singers, which I started seeing them as gods and goddess that she worshipped truly in her heart. Well, she was my in home-provider caregiver, but she was not doing right by it, and God caused some havoc for him to move me.

I left and returned to the streets of Skid Row, and like I said, I wanted to die. I really didn't care, and when Satan rose up in the girl I met downtown, I really prepared myself to die. I had already began using drugs again. I slept on the streets. I didn't go to dialysis for over two weeks period of time, then some days, I couldn't go any further, and I would call the paramedic, and they would bring me to the hospital. The hospital would clean my blood, give me my high blood pressure medicine, and so on. I would sign myself against doctors' orders and leave and continue to use something down on me. If I die, being a confused spirit entered my mind, so I didn't know if I was going to heaven or hell.

I said to myself I was going to close that chapter in my life and called my son and come to find out they had been searching for me for quite some time, but it was God's timing that mattered. He found me, and I went back to my mother's house, and God did just as He said to my spirit. He healed my anger, hate, unforgiveness, and stifle.

My mother and I had a great relationship, as well as me and my children. I no longer wanted to die anymore I write poetry, and I design plants in baskets and pots. God put it in my heart to get a business license to sell them. This is talent He has given me. I don't have to prostitute or sell anything to buy drugs. It would be days, and I felt as though I was getting weary for doing good, but I knew the word tells us do not get weary in doing well, so God told Paul to tell us this. He knew we would get weary in doing good, but being obedient to the word, it leaves the feelings of weary. If we obey the world, God will help us and rescue us through His strength.

I lean on God's everlasting hands. Some days, Satan tries to tempt me mentally, but I would always respond and tell the devil no, and when the temptation is over, Satan flees out of my mind because I have no desire to use. I would receive God, and I would answer His calling, and He chose me because I answered and took heed to His correction. The kidney is to bring me back to God's laws on eating. He told me when He choose me not to eat the swine because He wanted to set me apart because I was raised on pork. God told me a pig eats his own bowel movement and anything unclean. That's why he said it was an unclean animal, and it becomes unclean in my body, but I compromised and still eat pork here and there until I learned to obey, but I didn't obey, and on the streets, when I had nothing to eat and pork was offered, I ate when I still should be obedient to His word, but today I waited on God no matter what it looked like, no matter how Satan tried to pressure me, no matter how long the test goes. I waited on God. I don't mind waiting knowing God have kept me alive and kept death and made death behave. I can't wait to see where God is taking me. I've come a long way the stages of life with Christ, and it was fun. You're probably wondering why I said it was fun because I laughed at Satan today, the sons of God, as well as the men of old. I see the spirit in men; they just look and keep pushing. They can't even wink at me. They know my flesh wouldn't get excited, not even the handsomest man. My flesh is pure. Today I praise God each round I go with by the tempter and pass the test he present to me, I go higher and higher.

The eagle, I go higher and high like the eagle that sows high above no longer do. I abide under the shadow of God's wings. I sow in the mist of God's sanctuary in God's will. Satan and his imps can't come near me, not even the beast of the fields I sow high and above.

Chapter 8

THE BIRTHING OF CHRIST

Well, I was led downtown among the unclean so God could create love in my heart for His purpose. God had to show me these people were His children as well as the Gentiles in the Bible. Nothing is new under the sun. I began to share my money I got from begging to the next begging man and the bomb. He changed my heart by causing me to walk in their shoes. God brought me down from the pedestal I was on. The love that was birth was Jesus Christ.

Before this took place, I was attacked by a dragon. This guy had seven spirits I believe, and I saw two heads in the spirit. Out of nowhere, he appeared to me, verbally attacking me with a deep anger. The word sprang up in me to let me know who he was and what it was all about. I would physically fall with his spirit trying to enter me and seemed to eat up my inward body parts. This dragon represented the dragon in Revelation who tried to kill the woman that was going to give birth to a male child, which was Jesus.

After she birthed Jesus, she was led to a place to be fed for so many days and years. That was so the birth of Jesus, which was love, and around the unclean after this. For two more years, I stayed on the streets and was well taken care by the people God ordained to give to me and feed me. No one can dissect God. His ways are sometimes unseen, but He make Himself known unto His prophets in visions and dreams. He speaks to them face-to-face. That is what God did.

I represented the children of Israel who God feed after the birthing of Christ because God took Jesus up with His Angels, and the eagle flew down and took the women to a place to be fed. The eagle represented the Spirit, and the man's character was symbolic for the evil dragon, which was defeated, "I Made It."

Now that Christ was birthed through me, I don't judge. You never know what God is doing in people. I don't fear of getting defiled by unclean spirits. I willing lay my hands on the unclean to cast out demons and to heal the sick. I am going to get revenge on Satan through Christ Jesus. I was amazed to see I was chosen in the last days to birth Christ spiritually. What an honor. We need love to enter the New Jerusalem and to enter in the kingdom of God. All those years, I didn't understand or even knew the root of my drug addiction. It was very the guy who walked me home. He was Satan's first weapon. I was bruised by these angels, and now I am healed from Satan's lies and deceit. I am purified by the blood. I feel as though I am a virgin ready with my lamp oil filled with oil, waiting on the bridegroom.

Chapter 9

NOT COMPLETE

Well, at this point of my life, God was not through with me being that He was showing me what was going on in my bloodline. I had to experience the truth. I recall God telling me the reason I could not conceive from the men I was dating such as having a relationship. He spoke to Israel and the woman. They could not marry the men that was of another nation, while God was bringing them through different nation, but the women disobeyed God. But God did not give up on Israel.

Every generation, God sought to find a woman that would obey Him to bring the children out who was sacrificed to demons that was born to these angels, so He had to show me why these men were men of old, who crept in the churches, who was really the disobedient angel who was chained down in dark places, but by the woman disobeyed God. These men began to multiply by the women who bore children from them still after God destroy the one from the beginning before God called Noah to build the Ark, but the angels were not destroyed. God still had a plan. So God caused me to go through and experience why He told them not to marry these men. Santa was crafty, but God allowed him to build the nation Babylon. Funny and strange, but it is the truth.

Children served was underground where the angel is in dark places and the children that was born to them. This is how the angels come out of the underground and fit in with other nation may sound, but it is the mystery. God showed me how the women were before. God showed me how this went on for decades. I stayed in captivity for a long time, and my mother used to make me feel as though it was me that wanted to do what I wanted to do and not serve God, and that is why God didn't deliver me from drugs, but somehow I knew that was not true, which caused me to think why they couldn't they hands on me and expel the demon in me. God said to me they have sin in them. They were religious ruler. They were not after God's heart. They wanted praise from people. That is why they could not feel what the people needed. They had no empathy.

Mind you, I was on parole, and God was showing me who these religious rulers were and how Gentiles became about parole agent was like wolf. Most of the people who was sacrificed to them knew what kind of demon they had in you, which they kept in you and sending you through a test, seeing if you could be strong fighter or whatever kind of weakness you had. That was against the law, but God used what they intended for the devil for the good of those who love Jesus. This was the captivity of Babylon.

All this was an organization built underground. I was running from my parole agent, and I prostituted to support my habit. Now there had to be a sex demon in me to connect with the parole officer's bait. Looks just like my parole agent. He led me in the alley and asked me did I wasngtwdc a dagte. The Holy Spirit quicken me and told me not to by showing in an approached vision that he came to connect with me, to track me down for my parole agent because they knew I prostituted. I got a way because actually God was trying to lead me out of Babylon prison. I have to say the Spanish people knew me somehow. They had a wall around me, and there were watchmen. They held the police back until I went wrong my covering. I would lose, but God caused me to because I was not complete. It was told in the word of God that it was forty years when the Israel suffered until God rose Moses up, and it reminded me as I write. It was in my childhood that God had started revealing to me about the sons of God, the disobedient angels, and here is 2022, the year I am birthing this message.

Chapter 10

THE STAR, THE GODDESS,
AND THE SCAPEGOAT

After being in Downtown for some time, I met a guy who I began a relationship with. Before that, I remember he used to follow me Downtown and tried to approach me and offered me drugs for sex. I would get insulted and yell at him and tell him to get away from me. Actually he did not know he was insulting me because this is what they do Downtown, but I had a purpose. I was in a secret place with God. Jesus showed me this was end-time because he said the sign would be like Sodom and Gomorrah.

The beginning of knowledge is fear. I feared me because I saw the truth being revealed. I did not want to be part of the destruction. Well, one day, I gave him a chance to make himself known to me, and we began talking, and he explained to me he was going to a program (rehab). Later I discovered he had a sex problem. It was not the drugs he was addicted to, it was sex.

He took me to this hotel called Olive Hotel. He took me to this one room where there was a girl and a three-year-old and this guy who he introduced to me. The guy represented Lucifer, the girl represented the goddess, and the child was the scapegoat who was sacrificed. I recognize that they were not in the system, children service, and I wonder why because for sure everything that was going on in that hotel was illegal. I later found out that that hotel was close down, and the police knew of it, but they did not have authority to enter. They kept the entrance to the door lock, and that was when the word of God began to reveal it was ran by a satanic organization, people who worshipped Satan. The people who were in and out of their apartment got high and bought drugs in the building.

The little boy stayed undress all day long, talking to himself and playing by himself and doing strange things, and his so-called parents would sock him really hard, never really explaining to him that what he was doing was wrong and why he shouldn't do such a thing. In other words, teaching him. I said to myself, *This can't be their child.* The child had to be really confused, and that is exactly what the devil wanted. The men who would go over there to get high, and the child was the prey, and they were Satan's advocate, causing the child to beat by the women and the man.

I never saw them take care of the child's physical needs. The word of God would sprang up in me and said, "There are jewels in dark places," and that child was a jewel. God showed me what He was saying to me about how the system took our children and sacrifice them to demons and how Babylon was from the child looked exactly like my second son. There is a mystery about him and my son that I can't reveal. These demons knew how to program this child to do whatever they wanted him to do.

Babylon built her system of stolen children, which had been going on for centuries until God got ready to bring Babylon down and reveal the truth. Her watchmen were vicious dogs, her probation officers were demons, and they knew how to set you up to get you arrested. They knew it took God Himself to deliver you from them. The word of God said the truth would set you free, and God revealed the truth to me, and I fought with His revelation and knowledge. I would expose them in heaven and on earth. God was ready to deliver me out of the hands of Babylon's captivity and set me totally free from prison walls and redeem my children, but the battle didn't stop. Saint Jude prepared me in his footnotes that I had to fight. He also spoke how there were certain men of old who crept in the church, and to the grace of our Lord and Savior Jesus Christ, into lasciviousness and denying the only and true God. These men were ungodly men.

I recall having a relationship, but this guy was being exposed exactly what Saint Jude was speaking about all. He was interested in sex and to cause me to lose my faith and my soul. I lived in a tent, and he was supposed to be my boyfriend to protect me, but when I refused to have sex with him, he would get mad and leave. When another man would disrespect me, he would not defend me. This is when the word of God became living, how this men turned the grace of God to lasciviousness. They had no mercy for me. They knew I worship Jesus, and they felt I was caught in sin by them. They didn't care to protect me. The word of God said every nation, race, color, and creed go back to their homeland and escape. If they didn't escape Babylon, they would suffer in her bed of immorality. These men knew I was chosen, and I suffered.

Chapter 11

THE BATTLE WITH THE STRONGHOLDS

Fight contends! Do battle! When apostasy arise, when false teachers emerge, when the truth of God is attacked, it is time to fight the fight of faith. Only believers who are spiritually "in shape" can answer the summons. At the time, beginnings of Saint Jude letter he focuses on the believer's common salvation, but then false teachers have crept in to the church, turning God's grace into dealings with unbelieving Israel, disobedient angels, and wicked Sodom and Gomorrah. In the face of such danger, Christians should not be caught off guard. The challenge is great, but then God is able to keep them from stumbling. There are some people who would try telling me that this was not so, but we see as Saint Jude's prophecy plainly state it is true. I had to fight with the sons of God, disobedient angels that rose up.

In my children, I had to constantly present the word to them by correcting them with Jesus's teaching and the word of God. I had to plant seeds of faith in them. Satan want their soul because of the first men who disobeyed God and married the women God told them not to. Israel was Hebrews, and Hebrews were not supposed to marry Gentile women, but God had another plan. He called certain women that was born in the tribe of Hebrew and that was Gentile. I discovered I was being chosen to a royal nation, Israel. God spoke to me and told me not to eat the swine just as He ordered the women before me not to marry the men God knew was sons of God in darkness that crept into the churches. He ordered them not to marry.

God did not have to explain to those women that these men were disobedient angels. Those women were supposed to be obedient. Even I fail into disobeying God, but it went through the bloodline without knowing the truth or even tried to teach the truth. God was looking to break this curse and seek a woman to be unwed in this bloodline, but he plainly said in the New Jerusalem there would be no lasciviousness, no dogs, and no thieves. God is going to raise up a generation of young men and women who is seeking him and not each other married unto him only.

Well, I had my sons jump on me, but I didn't give up. I constantly preached to them, and they would bring up my past. I had a son who would say white men wrote the Bible, and he would seek other religions, and I would tell him who Jerusalem was, and I would explain to him who Jerusalem was. He was a half-breed mix. His mother was a Haitian, which black was the color of Africa American, and her father was a Amorite, which is the color for Caucasian.

Jerusalem was a chosen nation of God. Israel was Hebrew but dark-skinned as though the color of Africa America with course hair. I had to open their eyes to false teaching and hear say knowledge that was not so. I had to watch my children disobey the word of God. They knew they were not supposed to tattoo their bodies. They still seek worldly things. I have to confess I disobeyed as well, thinking I could win a soul by fitting in. It was hard to correct a child when he sees you did the same thing. I just had to be honest with them about my mistake.

My mother took every last one of her grandchildren from birth, which I had two other sisters who lost kids as well in the system. We all were close. This is how the system caused my grandmother to believe they was doing the right thing, but they were taking power and authority over the family and curse them while they were destroying the mother who birthed them and eventually destroying the children they birthed, but God is awesome. He prepared my mother, the head who Satan wanted to destroy. He thought he would do it because my mother, I believer, should have never married my father. I was told her parents' ways were strict, and she wanted to leave her family, so she got married to my father. He was Satan's advocate. My mother divorced my father, and she never went into the world; she kept singing in the choir and playing the piano since I was a baby.

I am sixty-two, and my mother is eighty-three. I remember when I was really seeking Jesus before Jesus introduced me to God. I read in the Bible in prison that Satan was going to attack this woman's off-spring to try and get to the head, my understanding. He was doing that through my mother's children and grandchildren. My mother is who Satan is after. She is over eighty years old as I write. She got a doctor's degree in theology. She wrote a book called *Exploring Family Curses*. She was a correctional officer and retired parole officer. Now it might be hard to believe, but God established my mother financially to take care all of her children. I believe God is going to let my mother see the promises He promised her and let her see her children and her grandchildren well established before he would take her.

My mother is healthy. She walks fast and drive. She owns a women sober living home and still very active in the church. She still have to be insulted by Satan's strongholds through her grandchildren as well. All my nieces are grown, and I have to tell you I am and still overwhelm to see their body tattooed up with worldly things, and they know God. They were brought up from toddler in church, but God is not overwhelmed. His word and revelation are standing tall. The stronghold is bold, and they will fight you just as Saint Jude said. It is dangerous, but you must fight. They worship gods in their hearts; it is going on in church.

Babylon built her system and caused many people to be confused about who they were. Black people would call white people blue-eyed devils. They believed white people was Satan. I had a supervisor who was white and was from Africa and was born in Africa. Satan tried to make me believe God didn't ordain me to write this revelations and knowledge and chose me to be set apart. I remember being in prison, and I read the New Testament over and over, hoping it will help me give up drugs and be delivered from my drug addiction, but every time I get out, I go right back to drugs, but I didn't fully understand what my purpose in my life was, and I had to experience these things.

God wanted me to know what was going on in my bloodline in order for Him to equip me to fight and to hate the very sin that was used to enter my bloodline (lasciviousness), which is what the sons of God used along with drugs to seduce women on the streets, and most of these women were from broken homes and unwed mothers.

One time, I went to jail, and something, the inner voice, told me to read the Old Testament to meet my God. I obeyed, and that is when I came to know God, and I learned God was so loving and kind and merciful. He was nothing like my family would cause me to believe. They caused me to think everything I did, I would go to hell if I did not stop in my on strength. I came to find out whose God's chosen people was. Jerusalem spoke loud in my inner men. I knew God was trying to tell me something, then I came to the part where He spoke about the things He told Israel. They could not eat when I read that my spirit absorb it, and God was telling me not to eat the swine, something I eat all my life, but I obeyed for many years.

God called me and chose me as He did with the Israeli, the Hebrews, to be set apart of the royal nation (Israel). I constantly continued using drugs, so I began to believe God was not choosing me, and I started eating pork skin and so on, but I was being under a test with just seeing if I believe. God was calling to set me apart. That is where Saint Jude spoke in his footnotes how unbelieving Israel had to fight because there is still some people of Israel eating pork because of Paul's teaching, people believed because Paul taught how we should not say what is unclean, and they felt it is okay to eat what God told Israel not to eat, it is okay. God told Israel not to because they were chosen as a royal nation, just as he told Adam and Evil not to eat of the certain tree in the garden, just as he told Saul to kill everything. We have to understand that if God told you something to do or not to do, it's for you not to compromise. This is how Satan will trick you.

Obedience is better than sacrifice. The word *obedient* means "complying or willing to comply with orders or requests; submissive to another's will." God and I came to find out when you eat anything unclean, it becomes unclean in your body. That is where diseases come from if you know the word. God was preparing Israel when He was bringing them out of Egypt. He gave them the commandments and ordered them not to eat certain foods and told them to obey, and if they would obey His ordinance and commandants as they travel.

Those uncurable disease that God cursed the other nation with those disease would not come upon them. This is what was going on. Now as I write, God was giving Israel and His chosen people a chance to return to Him and be healed by returning to His ways. That is why there is so much sickness, new disease like COVID, and diseases before that Paul was teaching to the Gentiles, but God's plan was to bring the Gentiles up to a royal standard with Him because they did not reject Jesus Christ. They accepted Him. He was going to wean them, slowing off unclean thing just as He had to do to me.

We are not supposed to put stumbling block in front of people. So I had to fight strongholds with the revelation and knowledge God gave me that came to pollute what God ordained me not to do. I had to trust God to deliver my children out of the strongholds. I had to return back to the commandments of God and reject unclean food and come out of Babylon ways. That is how I was going to escape her. She built her foundation on booze, drugs, and sex, and a lot of shelter they have for homeless. They sell drugs to keep it funded. This is Babylon ways, and that's how she kept the prison walls up and make her money with different nations as well.

There is a church undercover that had a drug house that sell drugs to keep their church in function because these pastors want praise from people about their good work in community. God did not ordain them because God told Solomon go to the governor and tell him to give to Solomon a certain amount of gold, etc. to build His temple, and when Solomon repeated everything that God said, the angel that stood in front of the governor gave to Solomon he knew it was of God because Solomon said everything God told him to tell the governor anything of God, He will bless and don't bring any sorrow to it. God was telling His people to come out of Babylon by not partaking in her ways.

Chapter 12

FIRST TO SERVE

I was accepted in a Shelton call first to serve the reason why my last experience of getting arrested and going to jail. I got probation, and they put me in a Shelton, and the Shelton agreed to find a place of resident for me within three months upon agreement with the courts to get me off the streets, being homeless, but everything I went through was protocol ordained by God. Strange, but it's true. God used me to change the law and expose Babylon, her policemen, her workmen or security guards (watchmen). God said they were like vicious dogs, and there were her parole agents. I would catch them in tents, getting high and trying to set their next victim up, how she built her establishment on booze, sex, and drugs and how the people they had on the streets were the prey and sacrifice to them why.

I was using the prophecy of "God was ruling my spirit." I would speak what God was telling to speak me under the influence because I was baptized with the Holy Spirit and drunk with the Holy Spirit, and God took the foolish thing to confirm the wise, and it was the time God was going to make himself known to me, that he was telling me these things to say. I went to buy three five-dollar cocaine rock and did not know the police was watching me. I asked this guy if he could help me carry this bag to my tent (someone gave me a bag of clothes). He agreed if I agree to give him some cocaine when we got to my tent. I passed him a five-dollar piece of cocaine, and the police pulled up and jumped out of their car and tried to grab my hand and take the cocaine out of my hand. I fought them, then they kept telling me to give it to them. I would get out on a OR, but I did know

God did change the law through my prophesying because actually God used the police who were righteous to arrest me. I finally gave them the dope, and I could not cry for some reason.

My breastplate was on. I just accepted what happened, being that it was a felony, and you can get prison time for possession of dope, and there were people who God was preparing all the time that had a heart to hear what I was saying, policeman and great people in authority, because God would use me, and I would go on the corner uptown where the people who were lawyers and district authority. They actually were listening to me preaching the prophecy God gave me about downtown Babylon. They booked me in, and later they did sign me out, and that was not supposed to happen. I had a record as long as my arm since. I was eighteen years of age, and I was in my early fifties when they released me. I still didn't really know if it was God's doing or what the world would say luck because I had to go to court.

Well I, went to court, and the judge gave me summary probation where I didn't have to report to anyone, and I was told by the lawyer they couldn't imprison anyone for possession anymore, just sells because the system undercover was exporting drugs through and putting it on the streets and arresting the buyer and user. They changed the law I saw God.

God has a nation He is delivering off Babylon's potion of immorality crack cocaine. Well, in this Shelton, I was ready to file a lawsuit about them taking my daughter illegally, being there was lawyer who could not take the case, afraid they would be stepping on someone's toes. Mind you, I had a degree already in law. I was going to file it myself. Well, this was not in the plan of God before I moved Downtown and became homeless. This was what God's will was. He wanted me to see Babylon's house of demons in full flesh when *relapse*, "For the Lord God does nothing without revealing his secret to his servants the prophets" (Amos 3:7).

I didn't understand why I thought I was complete, so I asked God why He spoke and told me they were going to try and defile me. I still didn't understand. I never thought I was perfect. I kept my eyes and my heart on Christ, but I came to find out I had people who knew I was chosen and set out to deceive me. They were not in my best interest.

Family members as well as church friends worshipped Satan in there heart, and God exposed them. Downtown I was overwhelmed when He pulled them out of the church in their first estate (bodies). If God has chosen you, He would build and let you see everything that was set up. It was set up just to bring you through. The woman pastor I met, her body was defiled by these men. They knew my body was not defiled. They knew the truth, and they didn't teach the women the truth. They taught what they fell into sex without marriage but self-conscious. They knew they were deceived by disobeying.

I had a pastor who was giving me marriage counseling and told me I should treat the guy as if he was my brother and share with him, but I could not because God got my attention about Jerusalem, how He gave her the best of everything, and everything He gave to her, she gave to all the men she went to bed with. She didn't know that word was deep-rooted in me. I knew I was not supposed to give to a man what God gave to me as a women. When I was homeless Downtown, God used a store manager to bless me, and the guys Downtown tried to make their girlfriend believe I was trying to get at their men because the guys knew I was not into them. I stood out because I didn't do as the women did downtown, play house. I would tell the women I don't want your men. You are playing house. I am in a crisis.

In the women's heart, the men was being worshipped by them little gods. Well, in this Shelton, I was put in a clean room, and I gained the gift to design plants in flowerpots, so I kept myself busy making flowerpots to put in my apartment that the Shelton was going to prepare for me and to stay off drugs. Well, as time went by, I noticed they put a girl in my room as my roommate. She asked me what was my poison such as what drugs I used. God revealed to me a test she came to tempt me. I fell right into Satan's hands through her. We started using in the room, but she was exposed to be the workman of the supervisor over the program, Satan's advocate. She was placed there to cause them to trap me.

Also, once I started smoking with her, she informed the director over the program. I was using everyone that was being used by the director as an informer that got high and would break the rule and come in our room and use. No one would get in trouble but let me went out of the room after hours. We were not supposed to, and I get put on camera for breaking the house rules. God let me see first to service and was prepared for me a stepping stone when they would leave out of the room by morning, which I was worried because the room would have a foul smell, which was the scent of demons.

When they would leave the room, the room returned to its pleasant scent it had, and my plants was not scorched. Then my eyes were made open. I was not part of Babylon, a demon. I was stolen and sacrificed just as my children were through my father. "I myself will set my face against that man and will cut him off from among his people because he has given one of his children to Moloch, to make my sanctuary unclean" (Leviticus 20:3). I believe this happened through many generations, and they were trying to defile me and my dwelling place as God put in me such as He taught Israel's priests.

I read a book that God allowed me to receive in jail, and it was written by a priest. I found myself interested in it, and I checked it out and read, not knowing it was going to be of some help to me. This priest Satan was after to defile him, but Satan could not get in, so Satan attempted to get in and went to the priest's door and ring the doorbell, but this priest knew it was Satan. He told Satan to take off his shoes, but Satan refused somehow. The priest would identified Satan by his feet. I learned demons don't have toes, so Satan sent the demons through a spiderweb through the priest's house to get in to defile the priest.

This is what God was telling me. They wanted to defile me, people who knew I was chosen, to come out of them. I was a scapegoat as well as a sacrifice to demons, and it was a battle. The demons didn't want to let go. They lived in my body for a long time like I said. Parole officer were imps in Babylon's system. They knew God would have to set you free. Well, they kept making excuses why they were changing my room, and finally they put me in a room that the shower was messed up, and the room and beds were all torn up. God opened my eyes again to see that what He was saying to me, that no weapon that was formed against me shall prosper, but me being disobedient, God allowed me to experience that unclean spirit lasciviousness that entered the bloodline through sons of God.

God told me if I return back to Him and all His ways and commandants and obeyed His voice, He will deliver me out of Babylon's captivity, and He will return unto me and gather where He scattered me and my children. "And he said he will circumcise my heart and my seed heart (children) and he was going to cure my enemies and them that hated me and persecuted me and it was the church folks even as I write (praise God) And he said he was gone to make plenteous in every work (amen)" (Deuteronomy 30:3).

Chapter 13

THE CONFESSION OF A POET

I must admit I can't find fault in the women who were chosen before me to be unwed, married unto God only who fell into disobedience and got married to the men God ordered them not to marry. I knew the voice of God. I rebelled as well, but I thank God that He is a loving God, and He still had a plan to use me.

I hope this book would mainly reach the young generations, and they would seek God's face in all of what they do and not seek relationship in each other. Seek to please God Himself and to please God only. I confess the stronghold that I mainly had to fight the confusion in my mother's house, which was Bolivia Babylon, its birth name. I struggled to come out, but suffering is what God saw fit for me. If I suffer, I shall reign with Him the scapegoat (a goat sent into the wildness after the priest chief had symbolically laid the sins of the people upon it). As I was sacrificed to save all my family members, I forgave even when the battle of the stronghold. I had to fight, and being that my mother dealt with Babylon.

For many generations, she didn't understand me. She didn't realize she had strongholds, but she kept being who she was called and chosen to be to save her family until God rose me up and out of Babylon's sins. Such as the women in the church, the definition of a scapegoat is to blame a person for something even though it wasn't their fault being that I can identify the Holy Spirit in me. I heard the voice of God, but I wondered if they heard God's voice when He spoke to them and told them to reveal the truth, and they didn't do so.

Chapter 13

CONFESSION OF A POET

I must admit I can't fault the women who was chosen before me to be unwed marry unto God only who fell into disobedient and got married to the men God order them not to marry I knew the voice of God I rebel as well but I thank God is a loving God and he still had a plan to use me I hope this book would mainly reach the young generation and they would seek God face in all what they do and not seek relationship in each other seek to please God himself and to please God only. I confess the strong hold that I mainly had to fight who instrument all of the confusion in my mother house was Bolivia Babablyon birth name. I struggle to come out but suffering is what God saw fit for me if I suffer I shall reign with him the **Scapegoat— (a goat sent into the wildness after the priest chief had symbolically laid the sins of the people upon it)** as I was sacrifice to save all my family members I forgave even when the battle of the strong hold I had to fight and being that my mother dealt with Babablyon for many generation she didn't understand me she didn't realize she had so strong holes but she keep being who she was call and chosen to be to save her family until God rose me up and out of Babablyon sins. Such as the women in the church the definition of a scapegoat is to blame a person for something even though it wasn't there fau7lt being that I can identify the holy Spirit in me I heard the voice of God but I wonder if they heard God voice when he spoke to them and told them to reveal the truth and they didn't do so

About the Author

Melanie Goodall Hightower was born in Beaumont, Texas, to the parents Mr. and Mrs. Goodall. She attended elementary school in Beaumont, Texas, and later attended junior high school in Long Beach, California, then later graduated from Banning High school in Wilmington, California. Later she exceled and got her paralegal degree in law at Platt College. Melanie was only taken cared by her mother who clean rich Caucasian people's houses in the south. She was raised by one parent, her mother. Her father was taken off to prison when she was born. She later did meet him; she was about six year old, which you will discover upon reading this book.

Melanie was a very unique child. She was chosen by God and was protect by Him. As she looks back over the years of her life, she now can say that because Satan attacked her from birth. No one took notice that she was a special child. Melanie is very spiritual, and she knows God and have seen God face-to-face with His miraculous power. Melanie resides in Carson, California, with her family, who she loves watching. God proved His word through them. She loves music, writing, and praising God.